Contents

Introduction

■■■

If you are a member of the extended family of Internet surfers, you will have come across compressed files in ZIP, TAR and BinHex format, as well as other formats. These files were compressed so that they can be more easily transferred to other computers. To use them, you will need to decompress them with the appropriate software. This book will show you how to use the two main software applications:

- **WinZip** produced by Nico Mak Computing
- **PKZip** produced by PKWare, Windows version.

We will be using some technical terms, which we will now explain.

An **archive** is a file (not necessarily compressed) which groups together a number of files, possibly saved in several folders.

To decrease the size and therefore make file transfer easier, we use advanced compression techniques (especially on the Internet). Files whose size is smaller than the original size are called **compressed**. Usually these files cannot be used as they are. They must be converted with a decompression process. Nowadays, most compressed files are archives and therefore both terms tend to be used with the same meaning.

A self-extracting archive is an executable program which groups one or more compressed files. The original file is recovered with a simple double-click on the archive.

You must remember that shareware is not free. It is usually time-limited or has fewer functions than the complete version, with a few exceptions. If you use the shareware version of an application on a regular basis, you should register with the authors. This is the only way that shareware can carry on being developed and produce absolute jewels such as the ones we are going to show you in this book. To register, consult the sections "Buying WinZip" and "Buying the PKZip for Windows pack" in Chapters 1 and 10.

■ Symbols

Under this heading, you will find additional information.

This symbol warns you about problems you may encounter in certain cases. It also warns you what not to do. If you follow the instructions, you should not have any problems.

This symbol provides you with suggestions and tips: keyboard shortcuts, advanced techniques, and so on.

Part

WinZip

Whether you are a beginner in the art of working with ZIP files or you have been using compression software for several years, WinZip's intuitive interface should pose no problems. The authors have in fact designed two ways of zipping files: one specifically aimed at occasional users and/or beginners. The second, much more powerful, is specifically aimed at users who regularly create ZIP files or work with non ZIP archives.

1

Before you begin

This chapter will show you how to install, uninstall and download the latest version of WinZip. You will also discover its main features and various ways of accessing it.

■ The main WinZip features

These are some of the main features of the WinZip application:

- **Supports long filenames.** Archives compressed with WinZip do not truncate the long filenames often used in Windows 95 and 98.

- **Supports various formats of compressed files.** WinZip obviously supports the ZIP format. Therefore you can create ZIP files and extract the contents of ZIP files without an external program. On the other hand, if you want to compress and decompress non-ZIP files, you must have the appropriate compression/decompression software. This software will be used by WinZip, as if working with ZIP files. Please note that WinZip can decompress files in **TAR, CAB, Z, GZ, TAZ, TGZ, UUencoded, Xxencoded, BinHex** and **MIME** formats without requiring any external program.

- **Creates self-extracting compressed files.** WinZip can also create self-extracting archives. This type of archive is preferred if the end user does not have the relevant decompression software.

- **Works with antivirus software.** WinZip can work with antivirus software to detect possible viruses, before decompressing a suspect archive.

■ Installing WinZip

To install WinZip, follow these steps.

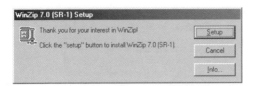

Figure 1.1   WinZip 7.0 is being installed.

1. Download the Winzip70 self-extracting archive (see section "Downloading the latest version of WinZip" below).

2. View the folder where you have saved the Winzip70 archive, for example, in My Computer or in Explorer.

3. Double-click on Winzip70.exe. A dialog box will tell you that WinZip 7.0 is being installed (see Figure 1.1).

4. Click on the **Setup** button. After a few seconds, it displays a second dialog box (see Figure 1.2).

Figure 1.2   Choice of installation drive and folder.

The Install to text box indicates the folder into which WinZip will be installed. If you want to install WinZip onto a different drive or into folder, modify the text box accordingly. Click on the OK button when you are satisfied with your choice of installation folder.

A third dialog box briefly describes the choices available in WinZip (see Figure 1.3).

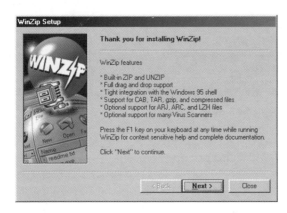

Figure 1.3 The main choices available in WinZip.

5. Click on the Next button and accept the terms of the licence agreement by clicking on the Yes button in the following dialog box.

6. WinZip can be used in "Wizard" mode (WinZip Wizard) or in "Classic" mode (WinZip Classic). Select the required mode in the following dialog box (see Figure 1.4).

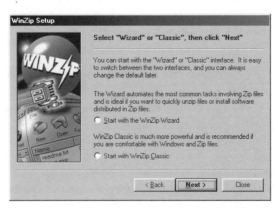

Figure 1.4 The two WinZip modes.

You should choose:

♦ **Wizard mode** *if you are only going to use WinZip to decompress archives downloaded from the Web or from CD-ROMs and to install programs contained in these archives.*

♦ **Classic mode** *if you want to create your own compressed archives and decompress existing archives. This mode is much more powerful, but it is also more difficult to learn.*

Starting in Wizard mode by default

If you have chosen to start in the Wizard mode by default (WinZip Wizard), the installation program prompts you to search for the ZIP files (see Figure 1.5). You may select:

■ The **Search Entire Hard Disk** option to search through all the folders in your hard disk or disks (see Figure 1.5)

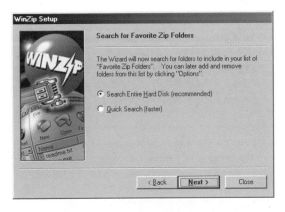

Figure 1.5 Searching for existing archives.

■ The **Quick Search** option to restrict the search to two predefined folders: **c:\cserve\download** and **c:\aol\download**. If necessary, these folders can be renamed and/or completed after installation. Refer to section "Modifying the Favorites folder" in Chapter 3.

*The search does not extend to the floppy drive, the CD-ROM drive and networked disks (if any). To find the compressed files saved on those media, use the **Search** button in the **WinZip Wizard** window.*

When the search is complete, the installation program gives you the number of compressed files found (see Figure 1.6).

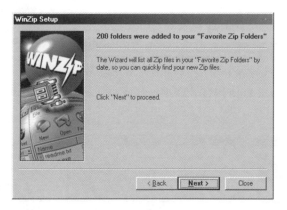

Figure 1.6   In this example, two hundred compressed files were found.

 *If the number of ZIP files exceeds 200, the program displays a dialog box like the one in Figure 1.7. Select one of the two options and accept the selection by clicking on the **OK** button.*

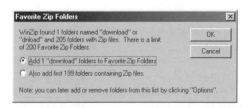

Figure 1.7   Unable to save all the ZIP files as Favorites.

7. Click on the **Next** button to terminate the installation. The installation program creates the **WinZip** folder in the **Start** menu and displays the WinZip Wizard window. You are now ready to work with the application.

Starting in Classic mode by default

If you have chosen to start in Classic mode by default (*WinZip Classic*), the installation program gives you two choices (see Figure 1.8):

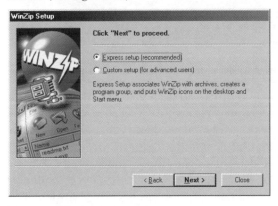

Figure 1.8   Express or customised setup.

■ **Express setup.** The installation program creates the WinZip folder in the Start menu and launches the WinZip application.

■ **Custom Setup.** A dialog box allows you to choose the installation options (see Figure 1.9):

   ■ **Associate WinZip With Archives.** If you select this option, simply double-click on a **ZIP, LZH, ARJ, ARC, TAR, TGZ, TAZ, GZ, Z, UU, UUE, XXE, B64, HQX** or **BHX** extension file in Windows Explorer or My Computer to open it in WinZip.

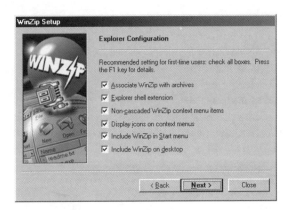

Figure 1.9 The installation options for WinZip in Classic mode.

- **Explorer Shell Extension.** If you select this option, one or more entries are added to the context menu when you click with the right mouse button on a compressed file.

- **Non-Cascaded WinZip Context Menu Items.** This option determines the display mode of the WinZip options when you click with the right mouse button on a compressed file. In this case, the options are displayed in the menu. If it is deactivated, the options are grouped under the WinZip command (see Figure 1.10).

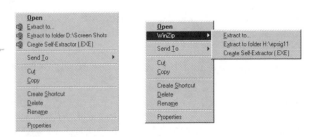

Figure 1.10 The context menu of an archive, with Non-Cascaded activated or deactivated.

■ **Display Icons On Context Menus.** This icon determines whether WinZip commands should be preceded by an icon when you click with the right mouse button on a compressed file.

■ **Include WinZip In Start Menu.** If you select this option, WinZip can be launched directly from the **Start** menu. Otherwise, you would need to select **Programs, WinZip** then **WinZip 7.0** to launch WinZip from the **Start** menu.

■ **Include WinZip On Desktop.** This option adds a WinZip icon to the Windows desktop. You simply double-click on this icon to launch the application.

 *All these options may be modified after WinZip has been installed with the **Explorer Configuration** command in the **Options** menu.*

The last installation dialog box prompts you to create the WinZip program group, with its associated icons, as well as an icon for the Self-Extractor Personal Edition program. Choose both and click on the **Next** button (see Figure 1.11). A last click on the **Next** button and WinZip is fully installed.

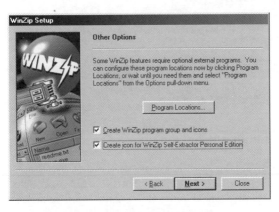

Figure 1.11 Creating program groups and icons.

■ Toggling between Wizard and Classic mode

As we have just seen, WinZip default mode is chosen at installation. But this can always be changed while using WinZip:

- To go from Wizard to Classic mode, click on the **WinZip Classic** button in the **WinZip Wizard** window
- To go from Classic to Wizard mode, click on the **Wizard** button on the toolbar in the **WinZip** window. If the bar has been customised and the button is not displayed, you can still use the **Wizard** command in the **File** menu or use the keyboard shortcut **Shift-W**.

 If you close the WinZip window in a different mode from the one defined at installation, a dialog box will ask you to confirm the execution mode you want to use next time you run WinZip (see Figure 1.12).

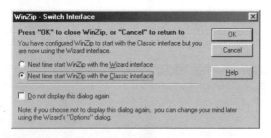

Figure 1.12 Selecting the display mode.

■ Uninstalling WinZip

Uninstalling WinZip is child's play. Check that the WinZip window is closed, click on the **Start** button and select **Programs, WinZip** and **Uninstall WinZip**. Uninstallation is carried out after you have confirmed it twice.

■ Downloading the latest version of WinZip

Version 7.0 SR-1 is the latest one at the time of going to press. It is possible that by the time this book reaches you, there may be a later version available. To make absolutely sure, check the **http://www.winzip.com/** Web site (see Figure 1.13) and click on the **Download Evaluation Version** link.

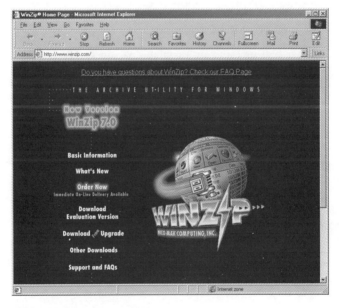

Figure 1.13 The WinZip Web site.

You will also find much useful information under the **FAQ** (*Frequently Asked Questions*) source site by clicking on the link **Support** and **FAQ**.

■ Starting and quitting WinZip

There are four ways of launching the WinZip application:

■ Double-click on the **WinZip** icon in the desktop

■ Click on the **Start** button and select **WinZip** in the menu

■ Click on the **Start** button and select **Programs, WinZip,** then **WinZip 7.0**

■ Double-click on a compressed file with the **ZIP, LZH, ARJ, ARC, TAR, TGZ, TAZ, GZ, Z, UU, UUE, XXE, B64, HQX** or **BHX** extension.

The last two methods are available whatever options were selected at installation. But if you had opted for starting in Classic mode at installation, the first two methods may not be available to you. Check the section on starting in Classic mode by default in this chapter for further information.

■ The WinZip window

WinZip is an **SDI** (*Single Document Interface*) application. In other words, you cannot open several archives at the same time within the same WinZip window.

In common with most Windows applications, WinZip has:

■ a title bar which shows the name of the open archive

■ a menu bar

■ a toolbar

■ a status bar.

The menu bar

The menu bar accesses all commands in the application. Please note the following commands:

- **Open Archive** and **New Archive** in the **File** menu, which allow you to open an existing archive and define a new archive, respectively

- **Favorite Zip Folder** in the **File** menu, which displays the Favorites folder

- **Convert** in the **File** menu, which changes the current archive to a self-extracting archive

- **Wizard** in the **File** menu, which provides access to the Wizard. Check the section on "WinZip in Wizard mode" in Chapter 3 for further information on the Wizard

- **Add** in the **Actions** menu, which allows files to be added to the current archive

- **Delete** in the **Actions** menu, which removes the file or files selected from the current archive

- **Virus Scan** in the **Actions** menu, which activates the execution of the antivirus utility associated to WinZip

- **Make .Exe File** in the **Actions** menu, which makes the current archive self-extracting

- **View** in the **Actions** menu, which allows you to view the highlighted file without having to decompress the archive

- **Extract** in the **Actions** menu, which unzips the files you have chosen

- **Test** in the **Actions** menu, which allows you to check the integrity of the files in the current archive

- **Configuration** in the **Options** menu, which provides access to the application settings

- **Contents** in the **Help** menu, which provides access to WinZip interactive help.

The toolbar

By default, the toolbar in WinZip has eight icons (see Figure 1.14).

Figure 1.14 The default toolbar in WinZip.

Icon	Equivalent Command	Function
New	**New Archive** in the File menu	Defines a new archive or opens an existing archive
Open	**Open Archive** in the File menu	Opens an existing archive
Favorites	**Favorite Zip Folders** in the File menu	Displays the list of Favorites, so it can locate commonly-used archives quickly
Add	**Add** in the Actions menu	Add one or more files to the current archive
Extract	**Extract** in the Actions menu	Extracts files from the current archive
View	**View** in the Actions menu	Displays the selected file using the associated program, an ASCII viewer built-in to WinZip or a program of your choice

Icon	Equivalent Command	Function
CheckOut	**Extract** in the Actions menu	Extracts the files in the current archive, creates a program group and places the icons for the unzipped programs and documents
Wizard	**Wizard** in the File menu	Activates WinZip Wizard mode

The status bar

The status bar permanently displays various information on the current archive:

- number of files and total size before compression
- number of selected files and total selection size before compression.

Please note the two coloured light icons at the bottom right of the window. The green indicator shows that WinZip is not active, and the red one that it is active.

The work area

The work area is located between the toolbar and the status bar. Several items of information (or fields) are displayed about each file in the open archive. Check the section on the display of the WinZip window in Chapter 4 for further information on how to choose the displayed fields.

■ Buying WinZip

Print the WinZip purchase order in the **Program Files\ WinZip\ORDER.TXT** file.

WinZiP's Web address is:

> **http://www.winzip.com**

WinZip is distributed in the UK by the US Distributor:
Nico Mak Computing
P.O. Box 540
Mansfield
CT 06268 USA
Email: help@winzip.com

2
What's new in version 7.0?

Support of CAB files

Sorting and filtering information fields

Printing data displayed in the window

Comments to a ZIP file

Tip of the day

Using a single-click

Customising the toolbar

A command language for WinZip professionals

Other improvements to WinZip

WinZip version 7.0 comes equipped with several improvements and changes for the better. This second chapter will be looking specifically at these.

■ Support of CAB files

Microsoft uses a format of special compressed files with the .CAB (*cabinet*) extension in most of its applications. WinZip version 7.0 is now able to view and extract all or some of these files. As an example, Figure 2.1 shows the files in the **DRIVER11.CAB** archive in the Windows 98 installation CD-ROM.

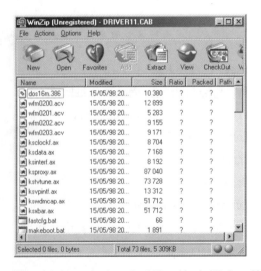

Figure 2.1 A sample view of a .CAB archive in Windows 98.

 Decompressing CAB files is certainly simple, but it requires serious know-how of destination and usage of the decompressed

files. For example, you might restore a system file deleted by mistake or because of a computer crash, or maybe recover and install a driver for a peripheral. But be careful, these operations are not for beginners and may well cause irreparable damage to your operating system...

■ Sorting and filtering information fields

The WinZip window displays one or more of the following items of information for each file in an archive:

- filename: **Name**
- file type, in full: **Type**
- date of creation and when last modified: **Modified**
- size of original file, in bytes: **Size**
- compression ratio: **Ratio**
- size of file after compression, in bytes: **Packed**
- CRC control value: **CRC**
- file attributes: **Attributes**
- file path: **Path**.

The information labels are displayed just beneath the toolbar.

If your screen resolution is set to less than 800×600 points, it is better to limit the display of some of these fields. Use the **Configuration** command in the **Options** menu. Select the **View** tab and choose one or more options in the **Columns** option group (see Figure 2.2).

*Even if all the information fields are not displayed, you can still call them up for a specific file. Click with the right mouse button on the file in the WinZip window and select **File Properties** in the context menu. A dialog box like the one in Figure 2.3 shows the missing information.*

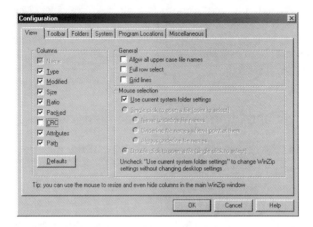

Figure 2.2 Choice of display of information fields.

This is not all that is new. Each field shown in the WinZip window may be used as a sorting criterion. For example, if you click once on the **Name** label, the files in the archive are sorted by name in ascending order. If you click again on the same label, the order is reversed: the files are now sorted in descending order of name. In any case, an arrow will show you the direction of the sorting order (see Figure 2.4).

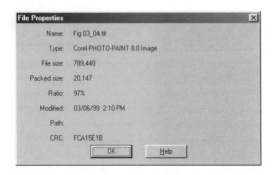

Figure 2.3 Complete information on file Fig 03_04.tif.

[Screenshot of WinZip application window]

WinZip (Unregistered) - Screen Shots.zip

File Actions Options Help

New Open Favorites Add Extract View Install Wizard

Name	Type	Modified	Size	Ratio	Pa
Fig 02_02.tif	Corel PHOTO-PAINT 8.0 Image	03/06/99 12:00 ...	199,366	91%	18
Fig 01_01.tif	Corel PHOTO-PAINT 8.0 Image	03/06/99 10:24 ...	186,504	91%	18
Fig 01_02.tif	Corel PHOTO-PAINT 8.0 Image	03/06/99 10:12 ...	141,974	95%	
Fig 01_03.tif	Corel PHOTO-PAINT 8.0 Image	03/06/99 10:34 ...	191,564	92%	15
Fig 01_04.tif	Corel PHOTO-PAINT 8.0 Image	04/06/99 9:43 AM	145,942	95%	
Fig 01_05.tif	Corel PHOTO-PAINT 8.0 Image	03/06/99 10:42 ...	146,250	95%	
Fig 01_06.tif	Corel PHOTO-PAINT 8.0 Image	03/06/99 10:45 ...	146,610	94%	
Fig 01_07.tif	Corel PHOTO-PAINT 8.0 Image	03/06/99 11:27 ...	159,058	95%	
Fig 01_11.tif	Corel PHOTO-PAINT 8.0 Image	03/06/99 11:28 ...	159,278	95%	
Fig 01_12.tif	Corel PHOTO-PAINT 8.0 Image	03/06/99 11:31 ...	73,904	95%	
Fig 01_13.tif	Corel PHOTO-PAINT 8.0 Image	03/06/99 11:41 ...	47,524	92%	
Fig 01_14.tif	Corel PHOTO-PAINT 8.0 Image	03/06/99 11:42 ...	99,864	92%	
Fig 01_15.tif	Corel PHOTO-PAINT 8.0 Image	03/06/99 11:44 ...	145,894	95%	
Fig 02_01.tif	Corel PHOTO-PAINT 8.0 Image	03/06/99 12:17 ...	185,174	96%	
Fig 02_05.tif	Corel PHOTO-PAINT 8.0 Image	03/06/99 12:30 ...	117,640	94%	
Fig 02_10.tif	Corel PHOTO-PAINT 8.0 Image	03/06/99 3:21 PM	185,842	94%	1'
Fig 02_12.tif	Corel PHOTO-PAINT 8.0 Image	03/06/99 3:22 PM	160,636	95%	
Fig 03_02.tif	Corel PHOTO-PAINT 8.0 Image	03/06/99 1:09 PM	173,470	94%	10
Fig 03_03.tif	Corel PHOTO-PAINT 8.0 Image	03/06/99 1:12 PM	147,762	94%	9
Fig 03_04.tif	Corel PHOTO-PAINT 8.0 Image	03/06/99 2:10 PM	789,440	97%	20
Fig 05_01.tif	Corel PHOTO-PAINT 8.0 Image	03/06/99 2:34 PM	161,148	96%	

Selected 1 file, 18KB   Total 45 files, 1 143KB

Figure 2.4 Files are sorted by name in ascending order.

If you prefer, you can also use a menu command to select the sorting order: Open the **Options** menu, point to **Sort** and choose one of the ten commands available. A tick mark appears in front of the field selected as a sorting criterion.

Please also note that the horizontal space attributed to each field can be freely adjusted. Move the mouse pointer to the right-hand end of the label you want to resize. When the pointer changes shape, keep the left mouse button pressed and move the mouse to the left or to the right to achieve the required size. Practice for displaying long names in full...

 If you double-click on the right of a label in the field, its space is automatically adjusted to the size of the information in the field.

■ Printing information displayed in the window

To help you see more easily the filenames and properties of the archives stored on your hard disk, you can print their contents. This is how you do it:

1. Open the archive whose contents you want to print.

2. Use the **Print** command in the **File** menu, press **Ctrl-P** or click on the **Print** button in the toolbar (this button does not appear by default. Check the section "Customising the toolbar" in Chapter 2 to find out how to display it).

3. Select the printer to be used in the **Print** dialog box and click on the **OK** button.

If you want, you can print the contents of an archive to a text file. For this, you need to install a generic printer "Text only" on your computer. Follow these steps:

1. Click on the **Start** button and select **Settings** then **Printers**.

2. Double-click on the **Add printer** icon. This displays a dialog box called **Add printer wizard**.

3. Click on the **Next** button.

4. Choose **Local printer** and click on the **Next** button. After a few seconds, the dialog box in Figure 2.5 is displayed.

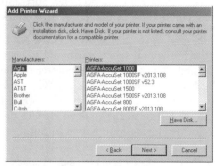

Figure 2.5 Choosing a new printer.

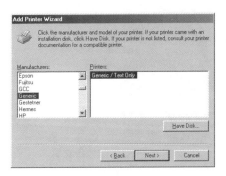

Figure 2.6 Selection of a generic Text only printer.

5. The list box on the right includes a list of manufacturers and the box on the left gives a list of printers offered by each manufacturer. Select the manufacturer **Generic** and the printer **Generic/Text only** (see Figure 2.6).

6. Click on the **Next** button. Now you must select the printing destination. Choose **FILE:** in the list box (see Figure 2.7).

7. Click on the **Next** button, name the printer and confirm. After a few seconds, the required drives are installed on your computer.

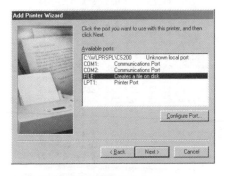

Figure 2.7 Printing a disk file.

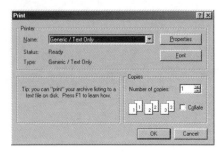

Figure 2.8 Printing a text file.

When you launch the **Print** command in the WinZip **File** menu, simply select **Generic/Text only** in the **Name** drop-down list (see Figure 2.8) and indicate the name and location of the resulting file.

This is an example of a file printed in this way:

```
08/12/98   09:56     C:\testssm\test2.zip          Page 1

Name                 Modified           Size  Ratio Packed
01-01.psp+           07/12/98 11:17   52 962   89%   5 815
01-02.psp+           07/12/98 11:18   63 659   89%   7 249
01-03.psp+           07/12/98 11:18  181 270   60%  72 510
01-04.psp+           07/12/98 11:19  190 792   61%  74 458
01-05.psp+           07/12/98 11:21  160 414   58%  67 857
01-06.psp+           07/12/98 11:28  152 023   57%  65 536
01-07.psp+           07/12/98 11:27   77 610   90%   7 615
01-08.psp+           07/12/98 11:30  156 274   57%  66 428
01-09.psp+           07/12/98 11:31  168 319   59%  69 215
01-10.gif+           25/02/98 15:37    5 427   13%   4 731
01-11.psp+           07/12/98 13:00  173 740   60%  69 801
01-12.psp+           07/12/98 13:05   98 132   88%  11 873
02-01.psp+           07/12/98 11:12  182 045   60%  72 822
02-02.psp+           07/12/98 13:42  227 872   66%  77 879
02-03.psp+           07/12/98 13:43  160 738   58%  68 275
02-04.psp+           07/12/98 13:44   87 332   90%   9 160
02-05.psp+           07/12/98 13:54  173 972   59%  70 690
02-06.psp+           07/12/98 13:55   98 850   89%  10 966
02-07.psp+           07/12/98 13:55  164 363   59%  68 170
02-08.psp+           07/12/98 13:57  130 659   87%  17 300
02-09.psp+           07/12/98 13:57  101 450   89%  11 441
```

```
02-10.psp+          07/12/98 14:02  118 829  88%   14 504
02-11.psp+          07/12/98 14:02   71 272  90%    7 344
03-01.psp+          07/12/98 15:33  110 255  76%   26 692
pkware mailing l... 07/12/98 09:27  230 708  82%   40 817
pkware newsgroup... 07/12/98 09:27  194 450  83%   32 848
winzip mailing l... 07/12/98 09:27  448 862  59%  181 941
27 file(s)                        3 982 279 69%1 233 937
```

■ ZIP file comments

WinZip version 7.0 allows you to enter comments in an archive. Very useful for providing information for the people who will be receiving your archive...

Use the **Comment** command in the **Actions** menu, press **Shift-G** or click on the **Comment** button in the toolbar (this button does not appear by default. Check the section "Customising the toolbar" in Chapter 2 to find out how to display it). Whichever method you use, a dialog box named **Comment** will appear. Type your comments. If necessary, change the display font and click on the **Save** button to save them with the archive (see Figure 2.9).

Figure 2.9 Entering comments into an archive.

The same technique will allow you to view and modify the comments associated to an archive.

■ Tip of the day

As opposed to several Windows applications, WinZip can display a tip every time you open it (see Figure 2.10). Until you become fully familiar with how the decom-pression software works, it is advisable to keep this function active.

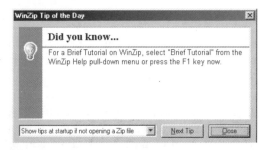

Figure 2.10 The tip of the day dialog box.

To deactivate the display of the tip of the day, select **Never show tips** at startup in the drop down list in the **WinZip Tip of the Day** dialog box and click on the **Close** button.

If you want to keep the tip of the day displayed, select:

- **Always show tips at startup** to display the **WinZip Tip of the Day** dialog box every time
- **Show tips at startup if not opening a Zip file** to display the **WinZip Tip of the Day** dialog box when you open WinZip without opening an archive.

Dialog boxes and the Wizard have a help button which allows you to identify the function of the controls included.

■ The single-click

If you use Windows 98 or if you have installed Internet Explorer 4.0 or higher under Windows 95, the Windows desktop and the behaviour of some applications (such as My Computer and Explorer for example) may be altered so that double-clicks can be replaced by single-clicks. This is similar to how hypertext links work on the Web. For this reason, Microsoft calls it "Web style".

To activate the Web style, launch the **Folder options** command in the **Display** menu of My Computer or Explorer. Select the **General** tab and confirm the option **Web style** (see Figure 2.11).

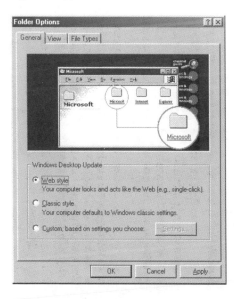

Figure 2.11 Activating Web style.

One click on the **OK** button and the general look of the desktop changes: all the shortcut icons are now underlined and
the pointer changes shape when placed on one of them. To
launch the corresponding application, now you only need a
single-click.

The same now applies to WinZip (see Figure 2.12).

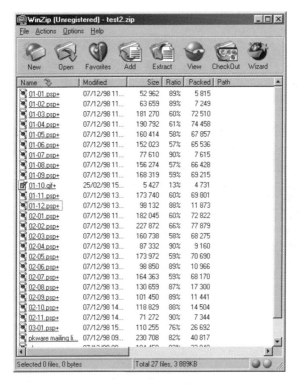

Figure 2.12 The WinZip window in Web style.

At this point, all you need to do to decompress one of the
files in an archive is to click on it.

If you do not like this way of working, you can restore the use of the double-click, without having to deactivate the Windows Web style display. This is how you do it:

1. Use the **Configuration** command in the **Options** menu.

2. Select the **View** tab.

3. Deactivate the **Use current system folder** settings option in the **Mouse selection** option group.

4. Select the **Double-click to open a file (single-click to select)** option and confirm by clicking on the **OK** button.

■ Customising the toolbar

If you want, you can customise the toolbar to simplify access to the commands of the most frequently used menus. To do this, you need version 4.71 or higher of **Windows Common Library** (COMCTL32.DLL). This library is an integral part

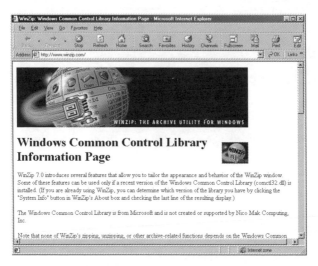

Figure 2.13 The Web site for downloading the Common Control 4.71 library.

of Windows 98 and of Internet Explorer 4.0. If you are still working in Windows 95, and do not have Internet Explorer 4.0 or higher installed on your computer, download the library from the Web address **http://www.winzip.com/ common_control_library.cgi** (see Figure 2.13).

 *To find out which version of COMCTL32 is in-stalled on your system, use the **About WinZip** command in the **WinZip Help** menu, then click on the **System Info** button. The last lines in the **View System Information** window will tell you what you require (see Figure 2.14).*

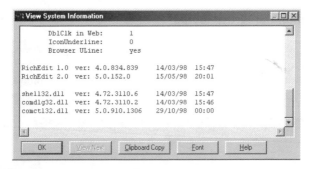

Figure 2.14 In this example, the COMCTL32 version is later than 4.71.

To modify the contents of the toolbar, click to the right anywhere on the toolbar and choose **Select Buttons** in the context menu. This displays a dialog box named **Select Buttons** (see Figure 2.15).

The **Available buttons** list contains all the buttons which can be placed in the toolbar:

 Displays the **ZIP Properties** dialog box which lists the information on the selected files in the archive.

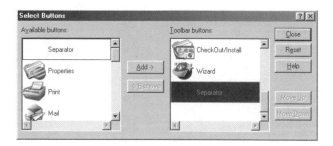

Figure 2.15 Customising the toolbar with Select Buttons.

 Prints a list of files in the archive to the printer or to a text file (check the section "Printing information displayed in the window" in Chapter 2 for further information).

 Defines a new email message and places the current archive in it.

 Provides access to recently used archives.

 Displays the **Delete** dialog box which allows you to delete a file, a file type, the selected files or the complete archive.

 Applies the antivirus utility installed on your computer to the current archive (check the section "Using an antivirus utility in WinZip" in Chapter 5 for further information).

 Creates a self-extracting archive from the current archive (check the section "Defining a self-extracting archive" in Chapter 5 for further information).

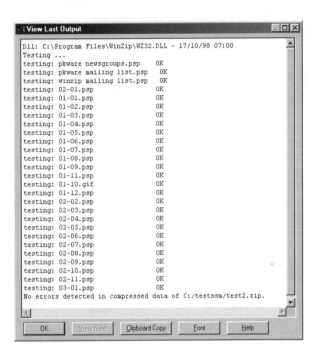

```
Dll: C:\Program Files\WinZip\WZ32.DLL - 17/10/98 07:00
Testing ...
testing: pkware newsgroups.psp      OK
testing: pkware mailing list.psp    OK
testing: winzip mailing list.psp    OK
testing: 02-01.psp                  OK
testing: 01-01.psp                  OK
testing: 01-02.psp                  OK
testing: 01-03.psp                  OK
testing: 01-04.psp                  OK
testing: 01-05.psp                  OK
testing: 01-06.psp                  OK
testing: 01-07.psp                  OK
testing: 01-08.psp                  OK
testing: 01-09.psp                  OK
testing: 01-11.psp                  OK
testing: 01-10.gif                  OK
testing: 01-12.psp                  OK
testing: 02-02.psp                  OK
testing: 02-03.psp                  OK
testing: 02-04.psp                  OK
testing: 02-05.psp                  OK
testing: 02-06.psp                  OK
testing: 02-07.psp                  OK
testing: 02-08.psp                  OK
testing: 02-09.psp                  OK
testing: 02-10.psp                  OK
testing: 02-11.psp                  OK
testing: 03-01.psp                  OK
No errors detected in compressed data of C:/testssm/test2.zip.
```

Figure 2.16 Archive integrity test.

 Creates a **UUEncode** file from the current archive. This type of files allows you to display a binary file in the electronic mail when the system used does not support binary files.

 Tests the integrity of the current archive. A window like the one in Figure 2.16 indicates the validity of each file.

 Views, adds or modifies the comments associated to the current archive (check the section on "ZIP file comments" in Chapter 2 for further information).

Provides access to the configuration dialog box (check Chapter 6 for further information).

 Displays the WinZip help overview.

 Closes WinZip.

The **Toolbar buttons** list box shows the buttons actually in the toolbar.

Using the buttons:

- **Add** to add the selected button in the **Available buttons** list box under the selected entry in the **Toolbar buttons** list box

- **Remove** to remove the selected button from the **Toolbar button** list box

- **Move up** to swap the position of the selected button in the **Toolbar button** list box with the one just above

- **Move down** to swap the position of the selected button in the **Toolbar button** list box with the one just below

- **Reinitialise** to restore the default toolbar: **New, Open, Favorites, Add, Extract, View, CheckOut/Install, Wizard.**

■ A command language for WinZip professionals

WinZip is a very powerful application, but like many other Windows applications, it can be pretty heavy to handle. If you carry out a large number of compression and decompression operations, you may want to talk to WinZip through a command language. You would then be able to

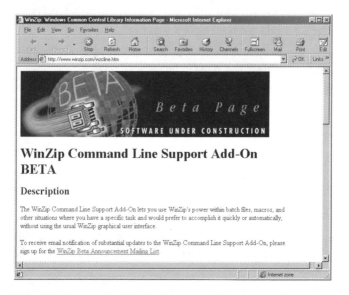

Figure 2.17 The download site for the command line support add-on.

define files to be handled in batches and macros to automate specific tasks, such as saving and compressing the documents you have been working on that day.

The command line/WinZip interface is in the process of final development. If you are interested in this, get on to the **http://www.winzip.com/wzcline.htm** Web site and click on **Download WinZip Command Line Support Add-On** (see Figure 2.17).

When you have downloaded the add-on, run it. When the installation is completed, there will be two new programs in the WinZip folder:

- **Wzzip.exe.** Command line compression program.
- **Wzunzip.exe.** Command line decompression program.

The use of these programs is shown in Chapters 8 and 9.

■ Other changes to WinZip

The improvements to WinZip do not end here. You will also see that:

- Compression to **ARJ** format allows the use of long file-names

- Most dialog boxes have a help function (top right) which gives you instant information on all controls in the dialog box

- If you select the **Move** option in the **Add** and **Drop** dialog box, the affected files are placed in the recycle bin rather than being permanently deleted. If you need them, this option can be modified. Use the **Configuration** command in the **Options** menu. Select the **Miscellaneous** tab and activate or deactivate the **Use recycle bin for move operations** option according to your needs.

For further information on improvements to WinZip version 7 and for answers to the most frequently asked questions, check out the **http://www.winzip.com** Web site and click on **Support** and **FAQ**.

3 Using WinZip

■ WinZip in Wizard mode

As we will see in the following pages, the WinZip Wizard mode is ideal if your only involvement with ZIP files is decompressing them and installing their contents. If on the other hand you also want to compress files and/or you want to work with archives of different formats (LZH, ARJ, ARC, TAR, TGZ, TAZ, GZ, Z, UU, UUE, XXE, B64, HQX or BHX), you will work in Classic mode.

Decompressing an archive with WinZip Wizard

When developing WinZip Wizard, the authors' main concern was to simplify unzipping and installing ZIP files.

If you have chosen to start in the Wizard mode by default, WinZip appears as in Figure 3.1.

Figure 3.1 The first WinZip Wizard dialog box.

After installing WinZip, you will probably have opted to search for .ZIP files in all the folders on your hard disk or disks (**Search entire hard disk** option). These files will have

Figure 3.2 This dialog box displays the ZIP files identified in your disk.

been placed in the Favorite folder. You can access them by simply clicking on the **Next** button (see Figure 3.2).

To decompress one of the ZIP files, simply click on its name and then on the **Next** button. The dialog box in Figure 3.3 is

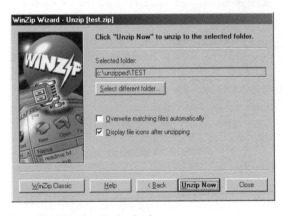

Figure 3.3 Selecting the destination.

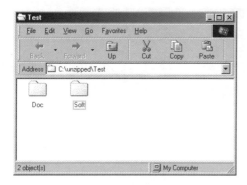

Figure 3.4 The folder containing the unzipped files.

then displayed. The **Selected folder** text box indicates the destination folder into which the ZIP file will be decompressed.
If necessary, select another disk and/or folder by clicking on
the **Select different folder** button.

Click on the **Unzip Now** button to unzip. When all the files
have been unzipped, they are displayed on the desktop in a
window on My Computer (see Figure 3.4).

To decompress a new ZIP file, simply click on the Next button and go through the same procedures as before.

Installing an application with WinZip Wizard

In the previous section, you have learnt how to use WinZip
Wizard to decompress a ZIP file containing data. Let us suppose now that the ZIP file contains an installation program
(such as **INSTALL.EXE** or **SETUP.EXE**). The Wizard automatically identifies the file and displays the dialog box shown
in Figure 3.5.

If the archive contains a documentation file, such as
FILE_ID.DIZ or **README.TXT,** simply click on the **View**

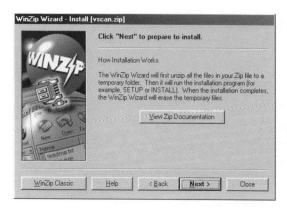

Figure 3.5 The Wizard has identified an installation program.

Zip Documentation button to display its contents. As an example, Figure 3.6 represents the FILE_ID.DIZ text file in the SCAN32.ZIP archive.

To install the application contained in the ZIP file, click on the Next button. When the files have been decompressed, a dialog box warns that the installation program is ready for execution (see Figure 3.7).

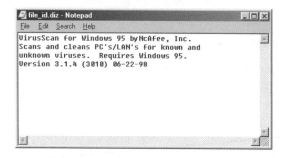

Figure 3.6 The SCAN32.ZIP archive contains a documentation file.

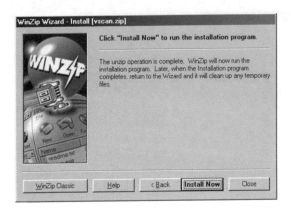

Figure 3.7 This message tells you that the installation program is run.

Click on the **Install Now** button and follow the instructions provided by the installation program.

Modifying the Favorites folder

To make using ZIP files simpler, the WinZip Wizard groups them in the "Favorites folder". The list of ZIP files is created initially at WinZip installation. If you have selected the **Search Entire Hard Disk** option, all your drives will have been scanned. If, on the other hand, you have selected the **Quick Search** option, only **c:\cserve\download** and **c:\aol\download** will have been scanned.

To modify the contents of the Favorites folder, click on the **Options** button in the first dialog box of WinZip Wizard. This displays the dialog box in Figure 3.8.

The **Favorite Zip Folders** tab displays the search path for the folders in which the WinZip Wizard looks for ZIP files. To remove a path, click on it, then click on the **Remove folder** button. To add a path, click on the **Add a folder to list** button and indicate the disk and folder you want to add to the list of Favorites.

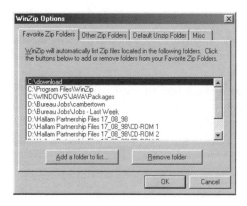

Figure 3.8 The list of folders scanned.

If you open a ZIP file whose path does not appear in the list of Favorites (for example by double-clicking on its name and moving its icon from My Computer to the WinZip Wizard window), the list can be completed automatically, manually or can be left as is. Select the **Other Zip Folders** tab and choose one of the three options on offer (see Figure 3.9).

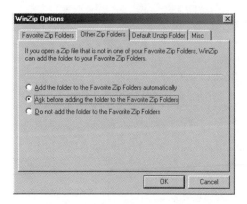

Figure 3.9 How to handle folders not present in the list of Favorites.

You will choose:

- **Add the folder to the Favorite Zip Folders automatically** to complete automatically the list of Favorites with all the new open ZIP files

- **Ask before adding the folder to the Favorite Zip Folder** where a dialog box will allow you to decide whether to add each new open ZIP files to the list of Favorites

- **Do not add the folder to the Favorite Zip Folders** if you do not want to add the new open ZIP file to the list of Favorites.

The **Default Unzip Folder** tab allows you to choose the default destination folder into which the WinZip Wizard will unzip the selected archives.

Finally, the **Misc** tab defines which of the two interfaces (*WinZip Wizard* or *WinZip Classic*) will be used next time you open WinZip (see Figure 3.10).

 By default, the WinZip Wizard searches for ZIP files in the paths listed in the Favorites folder. If you so want, you may choose

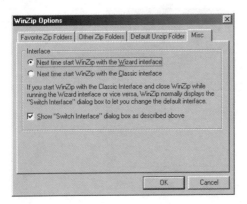

Figure 3.10 Choosing the type of WinZip interface.

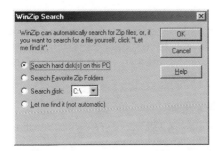

Figure 3.11 Four methods of identifying ZIP files.

another drive or extend the search to all local drives. Click on the ***Search*** *button in the dialog box named* ***Select Zip File*** *and choose one of the four options on offer (see Figure 3.11).*

■ WinZip in Classic mode

As you can see in Figure 3.12, the options offered by WinZip in Classic mode are much wider than in the Wizard mode.

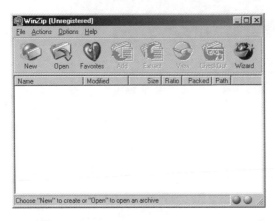

Figure 3.12: The WinZip window in Classic mode.

Let's remember that it is extremely easy to switch from Wizard to Classic mode: simply click on the **WinZip Classic** button. Conversely, to switch from Classic to Wizard mode, simply click on the **Wizard** button in the toolbar, use the **Wizard** command in the **File** menu or press **Shift-W**.

Viewing the contents of an archive

In My Computer, in Windows File Explorer or in any other file manager, identify the archive with the ZIP extension whose contents you want to view. Double-click on the file. The WinZip application opens automatically and displays the contents of the archive (see Figure 3.13).

If necessary, you may view one of the files in the archive by double-clicking on its name. This action opens the file in the associated Windows viewer. For example, if you double-click on a file with the .TXT extension, it will open in Notepad. If you click on a file with the .DOC extension, it will open in WordPad, and so on.

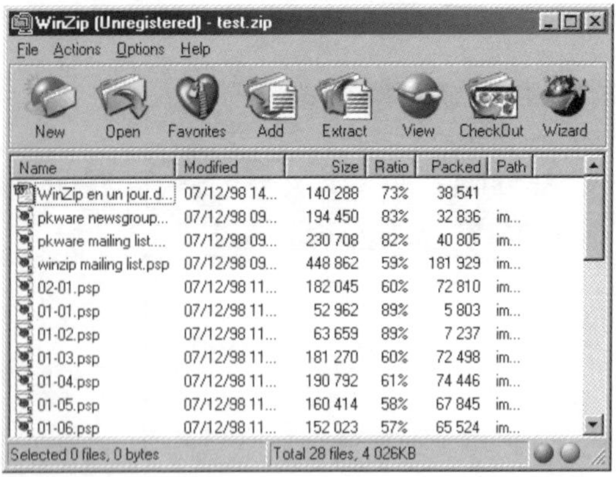

Figure 3.13: The contents of the archive are displayed in the WinZip window.

If you double-click on an executable file (.EXE, .BAT or .COM extension), it will be decompressed in a temporary folder and run.

When a file type is associated with a Windows application, it is preceded by a non generic icon in the WinZip window. To view a file not associated to any application, click with the right mouse button on its icon and select **View** in the context menu (you may also click on the file and use the keyboard shortcut **Shift-V**). A dialog box named **View** is displayed (see Figure 3.14).

Figure 3.14: The three viewing modes offered by WinZip.

Select the **Viewer** option and indicate the viewing program you want to use in the drop down list.

Another method for viewing an archive

If the WinZip window is open, you can still use Windows drag and drop function to view the contents of an archive:

1. Display the archive whose contents you want to view in My Computer or in Windows 95/98 Explorer.

2. Click on the archive, keeping the left mouse button pressed and drop the archive in the WinZip window.

3. Release the left mouse button. The contents of the archive are displayed in the WinZip window (see Figure 3.15).

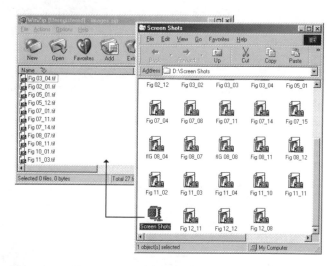

Figure 3.15: Using drag and drop in WinZip.

 *If you are not very good at dragging and dropping, you can also right-click the active icon in My Computer or in Windows Explorer and select **Open** in the context menu to achieve the same result.*

Decompressing an archive

As we will see, decompressing a file is a very simple operation. Locate the file to be decompressed with My Computer, File Explorer or any other file manager. Double-click on the file or drag it and drop it in the WinZip window, if it is open. This operation displays the contents of the compressed file. Click on the **Extract** button in the toolbar, use the **Extract** command in the **Actions** menu or use the **Shift-E** keyboard shortcut. Whichever technique you use, the dialog box in Figure 3.16 will appear.

Use the **Extract to** text box to specify the drive and the folder into which you want to decompress the archive.

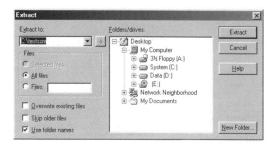

Figure 3.16 Choosing the extraction folder.

You may also select the destination folder in the **Folders/ drives** list box. If the destination folder does not exist, you can define it by clicking on the **New Folder** button. If necessary, select the **All Files** options in the **Files** option group, then click on the **Extract** button. Within a few seconds the files will have been decompressed in the specified folder.

 *If you want, you may extract only some of the files in the archive. Select the files to be decompressed. If the files are consecutive, click on the first one, keep the **Shift** key pressed and then click on the last file. If they are not, keep the **Ctrl** key pressed while clicking on the names of the files to be selected. Click on the **Extract** button in the WinZip toolbar. The **Selected Files** option is selected by default in the **Files** option group. Choose the destination folder and click on the **Extract** button. Only the specified files will be decompressed.*

Creating a new archive

To create a new ZIP file, you can:

- click on the **New** button in the WinZip toolbar
- use the **New Archive** command in the **File** menu
- press the **Ctrl** and **N** keys at the same time.

Whichever method you use, a dialog box named **New Archive**

■■

**Figure 3.17 Creating the IMAGES.ZIP archive in the root
directory of drive D:.**

will be displayed. Select the drive and the folder where you
want to save the archive and enter its name in the **Name** text
box. In the example in Figure 3.17, an archive named
IMAGES.ZIP is being created in the root directory of drive **D:**.

Click on the **OK** button. A new dialog box named **Add** is displayed. From the **Add** drop down list and the central box list
select the drive and the folder containing the files to be compressed (see Figure 3.18).

The **Action** drop down list indicates the action you want to
perform. In this case, you want to add the selected files to the
archive. If you want, you may also remove the original files
after entering them into the archive by selecting the item
Move Files from the list.

The compression ratio is chosen from the **Compression** drop
down list. The higher the ratio, the longer the compression
takes. The **Normal** setting is a good com-promise between
speed and compression ratio.

The table below provides an indication of the size of ZIP files
obtained by selecting the five suggested values in the

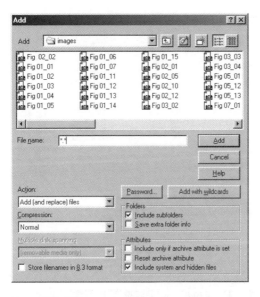

Figure 3.18: Adding a set of files to the archive.

Compression drop down list. The compressed files in this example are PSP images in 16 million colours, saved from Paint Shop Pro.

Compression in bytes	File size ratio	Compression type
None	3,984,919	0
Super Fast	1,392,434	2.86
Fast	1,311,176	3.03
Normal	1,236,253	3.22
Maximum	1,204,644	3.31

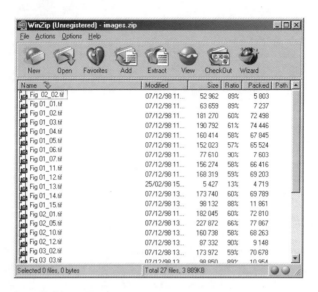

Figure 3.19 The WinZip window lists the files in the archive.

Click on the **Add** button. Within a few seconds, the compressed files have been created. The files contained will appear in the WinZip window (see Figure 3.19).

*If you want to, you can select all the files corresponding to a specified type. Enter the type in the **Name** text box and click on the **Add With Wildcards** button.*

*When the folders to be compressed contain one or more subfolders, you can choose **Include subfolders** and **Save Extra Folder Info** in the **Folders** option group to save the subfolders and their contents.*

In the example in Figure 3.19:

■ Twenty-seven files were placed in the archive

- The size of the files before compression is shown in the **Size** column. The twelve files have a total size of 3,889 KB

- The gain due to compression is shown in the **Ratio** column (between 13% and 90% according to the file)

- The size of the compressed files is shown in the **Packed** column.

If you want to know the total gain of space generated by the compression, use the **Properties** command in the **File** menu. This displays a dialog box named **ZIP Properties** (see Figure 3.20).

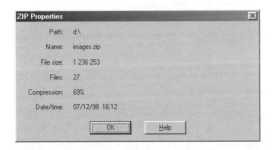

Figure 3.20: This dialog box displays the compression ratio as well as other information.

In the example in Figure 3.20, the space saved is only 69%. This is understandable, because the files in the archive are PSP images, already compressed by Paint Shop Pro. If you use WinZip to compress text files or uncompressed bitmap images, the space saved can, in certain cases, be huge: up to **98%**!

Adding files to an existing archive

In the previous section, you have learnt how to create an archive with WinZip. Let us suppose that you have forgotten

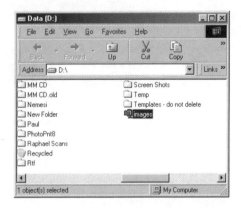

Figure 3.21 **Select the archive to which you want to add the files.**

to place one or more files in that archive. WinZip allows you to add these files very easily:

1. Click on the **Open** button in the WinZip toolbar and select the archive to which you want to add the files. In the example in Figure 3.21, it is the **IMAGES** file, saved in the **D:** drive.

2. Click on the **Add** button in the WinZip toolbar (you can also use the **Add** command in the **Actions** menu or the **Shift-A** keyboard shortcut) and specify the files to be added to the archive. Remember that:

   ■ To select consecutive files, simply click on the first file, then on the last one keeping the **Shift** key pressed.

   ■ To select files which are not consecutive, simply click on their name while keeping the **Ctrl** key pressed.

When you have selected all the files to be added, click on the **Add** button. The files are displayed in the WinZip window. In the example in Figure 3.22, three files have been added:

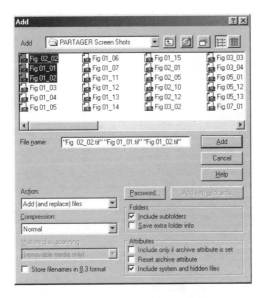

Figure 3.22 Adding three files to the archive.

Fig 02_02.tif, **Fig 01_01.tif** and **Fig 01_02.tif**. These files were created in Corel PHOTOPAINT.

Another way of adding files to an archive

Those of you who like drag and drop will be delighted to hear that this selection method can be used in WinZip to add one or more files to an existing archive. This is what you do:

1. Click on the **Open** button in the WinZip toolbar and select the archive to which you want to add the files.

2. View the files you want to add to the archive with My Computer or Windows Explorer.

3. Select the files by clicking on them, with the **Ctrl** key pressed.

4. Move the selected files to the WinZip window (see Figure 3.23).

Figure 3.23 Adding three files to the archive with the drag and drop method.

Removing files from an existing archive

Removing files from an archive is even simpler. Click on the **Open** button in the WinZip toolbar and select the archive from which you want to remove the files. Select the files to be removed by clicking on their name then press the **Del** key on the keyboard. This action displays the dialog box in Figure 3.24.

Having selected the **Selected Files** option, click on the **Delete** button. The selected files are deleted from the archive.

Figure 3.24 The Delete dialog box.

*To delete all files of the same type from an archive, you don't need to select them individually. Simply press the **Del** key on the keyboard. Select the **Files** option in the **Delete** dialog box and indicate the type of files you want to delete with the wildcard "**?**" to replace a single character and/or the wildcard "*****" to replace several characters.*

For example, you would key in:

◆ **.TXT to delete all files with the TXT extension*

◆ *ima?2.* to delete all files with five characters where the first three are **ima** and the fifth is **2**, whatever their extension.*

4 Configuring WinZip

- - - - - - - - - - - - - - - - - - - ■

The appearance of the WinZip window

Appearance and contents of the toolbar

Default folders

External access to WinZip

External programs

Other settings

Most of the settings for customising WinZip functions are grouped together in the **Configuration** dialog box. In this chapter, you will learn how to use this dialog box to get the best out of WinZip.

■ The appearance of the WinZip window

If the **Configuration** dialog box is not displayed, use the **Configuration** command in the **Options** menu. Click on the **View** tab (see Figure 4.1).

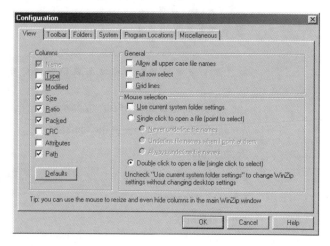

Figure 4.1 The View tab in the Configuration dialog box.

Information fields

The **Columns** option group includes nine options which define the information fields to be displayed in the WinZip window:

- **Name.** Filename (compulsory)
- **Type.** File type, in full

- **Modified.** Creation date or date last modified
- **Size.** Size of the original file, in bytes
- **Ratio.** Compression ratio
- **Packed.** File size after compression, in bytes
- **CRC.** CRC control value
- **Attributes.** File attributes
- **Path.** File path.

The **Defaults** button returns to the default display: **Name, Modified, Size, Ratio, Packed** and **Path** fields.

File display and selection

The General option group controls some details of file display and selection:

- **Allow all upper case filenames.** By default (option deselected), WinZip displays filenames as in Windows 95/98 Explorer. Note: if a filename contains upper and lower case characters, it is displayed as is. If it does not include upper case characters, it will appear in lower case apart from the first letter which is upper case. If this option is selected, files whose name are all in upper case will be displayed as upper case
- **Full row select.** By default (inactive option), only a file's Name field is a "sensitive" area. By this we mean that only by clicking or double-clicking in this field can you select a file. By selecting this option, the sensitive area is extended to all fields displayed in the WinZip window
- **Grid lines.** When this option is selected, the various information displayed in the WinZip window appears in cells, as in a table.

Mouse functions

Finally, the Mouse selection option group controls the mouse functions. We will now spend a few minutes on Windows

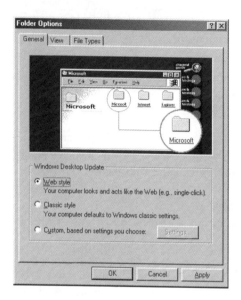

Figure 4.2 Web style activation.

display methods, so that we may gain a better understanding of the controls in this option group.

After the release of Internet Explorer 4.0, and with Windows 98, the Windows desktop has become "active". This means that you simply need:

1. to locate the mouse pointer over a file in My Computer or Explorer to select it.

2. to click on a file to run it (if it is an application) or to open it (if it is a document).

Double-clicking, which has proven so difficult for so many users, has been replaced by a simpler method. It is however still possible to use the old method (one click to select a file, two clicks to launch it or to open it).

To choose the mouse working mode, use the **Folder Options** command in the **Display** menu in My Computer or Explorer. Select the **General** tab to select **Web style** or **Classic style**, whichever you prefer (see Figure 4.2).

Let us return to the **Configuration** dialog box in WinZip. If the option **Use current system folder settings** is selected, the mouse works as it does in Windows (Web or Classic style). If you prefer, by selecting one of the two main options, you can choose to open files displayed in the window with a single or double click. Should you opt for Web style, choose one of the three options for underlining filenames (**Never, When I point at them** or **Always**).

■ Appearance and contents of the toolbar

If the **Configuration** dialog box is not yet displayed, use the **Configuration** command in the **Options** menu. Click on the **Toolbar** tab (see Figure 4.3).

The Toolbar tab allows you to define the way the toolbar will operate:

- **Use large toolbar buttons.** Choose this option to display large icons in the toolbar

- **Show button text.** Choose this option to display the name of each button in the toolbar

- **Show tool tips.** Choose this option to display help bubbles when the pointer is kept still over one of the buttons in the toolbar

- **Flat toolbar buttons.** Choose this option to make the buttons in the toolbar appear flat. Deactivate it to make them appear in 3D

- **Use high color toolbar buttons when possible.** Choose this option to give a better look to the buttons in the toolbar.

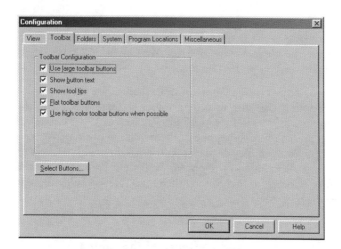

Figure 4.3 The Toolbar tab in the Configuration dialog box.

This only works if:

1. Windows is operating with a screen colour depth of over 256 colours (16, 24 or 32 bits).

2. The option **Use large toolbar buttons** is selected.

In the bottom part of the dialog box, please note the **Select Buttons** button which allows you to choose the buttons to be

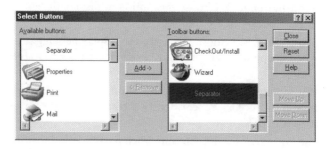

Figure 4.4 Choice and order of buttons in the toolbar.

displayed in the toolbar. Selection is carried out in the **Customise** dialog box in the toolbar (see Figure 4.4). You will be able to find out more about this dialog box by reading the section "Customising the toolbar" in Chapter 2.

■ Default folders

If the **Configuration** dialog box is not displayed, use the **Configuration** command in the **Options** menu. Click on the **Folders** tab (see Figure 4.5).

The **Folders** tab defines the default folders in WinZip.

Start-up folder

When you start WinZip without double-clicking on an existing archive, it will use a default start-up folder with the **New Archive** or **Open Archive** command in the **File** menu. This folder is defined in the **Start-up folder** option group.

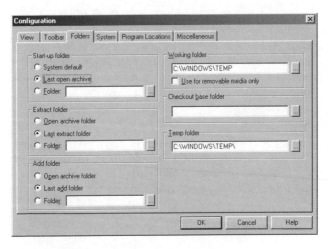

Figure 4.5 The Folders tab in the Configuration dialog box.

You can choose:

- The folder in which WinZip is installed, by selecting the **System default** option
- The folder in which you opened the last archive, by selecting the **Last open archive** option
- A folder of your choice, by selecting the **Folder** option. You can enter the path of the folder you want to use in the text box or you can click on the button with the suspension marks (...) to enter it more easily.

Decompression folder
When you click on the **Extract** button in the toolbar, WinZip suggests a default decompression folder in the **Extract** dialog box. This folder is chosen in the **Extract folder** option group.

You can choose:

- The folder which contains the open archive, by selecting the **Open archive folder** option
- The folder where the last decompression operation was carried out, by selecting the **Last extract folder** option
- A folder of your choice, by selecting the **Folder** option. You can enter the path for the folder you want to use in the text box or you can click on the button with the suspension marks (...) to enter it more easily.

Add folder
When you click on the **Add** button or when you move some files to the WinZip window to add them to the current archive, the **Add** window is displayed. This window shows a default folder which can be chosen in the **Add folder** option group.

You can choose:

■ The folder which contains the open archive, by selecting the **Open archive folder** option

■ The original folder of the last files added to a new open archive, by selecting the **Last add folder** option

■ A folder of your choice, by selecting the **Folder** option. You can enter the path for the folder you want to use in the text box or you can click on the button containing the suspension marks (...) to enter it more easily.

Working folder

When WinZip updates an archive, it creates a temporary file in the same folder as the original archive. If you are updating archives on floppy disks or on removable media which are almost full, there may not be enough free space. In this case, define the folder for storing temporary files in the **Working folder** text box. If you choose **Use for removable media only**, the folder will only be used for removable media. Temporary files defined for an archive saved on a fixed drive will be created in the same folder as the archive.

Default installation folder

If an archive does not contain an installation program, you can use the **CheckOut** button in the toolbar or the **CheckOut** command in the **Actions** menu to implement a simulated installation:

■ the files contained in the archive are placed in a folder of your choice

■ a program group will be created in the **Start** menu

■ a shortcut icon is created for each installed file.

The **CheckOut base folder** text box can be used to pre-define the default installation folder when you click on the **CheckOut** button.

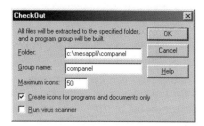

Figure 4.6 Using the pre-defined installation folder.

Let us suppose that you specify the **c:\mesappli** in the **CheckOut base folder** text box and that the archive you are working in is named "companel.zip". When you click on the **CheckOut** button to install this archive, the **CheckOut** dialog box suggests the **c:\mesapplis\companel** as the default folder (see Figure 4.6).

Temporary folder

When updating archives, WinZip creates a number of temporary files.

By default, these files are placed in Windows **\TEMP** folder. If the drive on which Windows was installed is full, you will get an error message about the creation of temporary files. If your computer has an auxiliary hard disk, define a path to the disk in the **Temp folder** text box (for example **d:\temp**) to get rid of these messages.

■ External access to WinZip

If the **Configuration** dialog box is not displayed, use the **Configuration** command in the **Options** menu. Click on the **System** tab (see Figure 4.7).

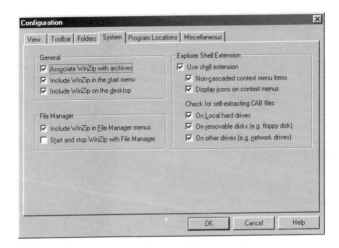

Figure 4.7 The System tab in the Configuration dialog box.

The **System** tab defines a certain number of options for accessing WinZip with My Computer and File Explorer.

General options

In the **General** tab, choose one or more of the following options:

- **Associate WinZip with archives.** When this is selected, double-clicking on an archive with the ZIP, LZH, ARJ, ARC, CAB, TAR, TGZ, TAZ, GZ, Z, UU, UUE, XXE, B64, HQX, BHX or MIM extension in My Computer or Explorer will open it in WinZip. Otherwise, Windows displays a dialog box named **Open with** (see Figure 4.8) where you must specify the application in which you want to view the archive

- **Include WinZip in the start menu.** Choose this to include the WinZip icon in the upper part of the **Start** menu

Figure 4.8 Specify the application you want to use.

- Include WinZip on the desktop. Choose this to place a WinZip shortcut icon on the Windows desktop.

File Manager

File Manager first put in an appearance in Windows 3.1. It cannot handle the long filenames of Windows 95/98. You can however still use it for all file compression operations carried out with WinZip. Specifically, you can:

- double-click on an archive to open it in WinZip, if you have chosen **Associate WinZip with archives** in the **System** tab of the **Configuration** dialog box
- drag an archive from the File Manager to the WinZip window to open it
- use the **WinZip** menu in the File Manager to open an existing archive, add files to an open archive, access the **System** tab in the WinZip configuration dialog box and the **About WinZip** dialog box.

The **File Manager** option group is aimed at those users who still have the old Windows 3.1 File Manager.

When the **Include WinZip in File Manager menus** option is chosen, the File Manager toolbar shows two new icons which allow WinZip to be launched and files to be added to the open archive in WinZip.

You can also choose **Start and stop WinZip with File Manager** to launch WinZip automatically every time you run File Manager. WinZip is also always ready for drag and drop operations with the File Manager.

 *To open File Manager, click on the **Start** button in Windows, select **Run** in the menu, enter the **Winfile** command in the **Run** dialog box and click on **OK**.*

My Computer and Explorer

The **Explorer Shell Extension** option group contains a number of options for managing the interaction between My Computer, Explorer and WinZip.

When the **Use shell extension** option is chosen, you can access several WinZip commands by clicking with the right mouse button on the file in My Computer and Explorer.

Choose **Non-cascaded context menu items** if you want the **Extract to, Extract to folder** and **Create Self-Extractor** commands to be immediately available in the context menu of My Computer and Explorer. If **Non-cascaded context menu items** is not chosen, these three commands are available under WinZip in the context menu.

The option **Display icons on context menus** determines whether an icon is displayed to the left of the WinZip commands in the context menu of My Computer and Explorer.

When you right-click an **EXE** file in My Computer or Explorer, WinZip examines its contents to see whether it is a

■■

conventional executable program or a self-extracting archive. If it is a self-extracting archive in **CAB*** format, the operation may take some time: up to 3 seconds on a floppy disk. If you want, you may deactivate the checking function for **EXE** files by deselecting one or more options in the **Check for self-extracting CAB files** option group.

* The CAB compression format is registered to Microsoft.

■ External programs

If the Configuration dialog box is not displayed, use the **Configuration** command in the **Options** menu. Click on the **Program Locations** tab (see Figure 4.9).

The **Program Locations** tab indicates names and settings for external programs used with WinZip.

The **Viewer** text box specifies the programs to be used when you double-click on a file whose extension is not associated

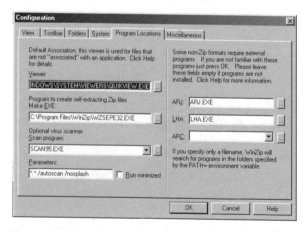

Figure 4.9 The Program Locations tab in the Configuration dialog box.

with any Windows application. This text box may contain one of the following programs:

- **QuickView**, if you have Windows QuickView installed
- **SCCVAPI.EXE** (*System Compatibility Corporation's "Outside In" file viewer*), if the program is installed on your computer
- **NVIEWER.EXE**, if the Norton Desktop for Windows application is installed on your computer
- **WNFV.EXE**, if the application PC Tools for Windows is installed on your computer
- **NOTEPAD.EXE**, if none of the previous programs were found.

The **Make EXE** text box contains the name of the program to be used for creating self-extracting archives. By default, this is the WZSEPE32.EXE program, which comes with WinZip.

The **Scan program** text box contains the name of the virus detection program installed on your computer. Go to the section on "Using an antivirus utility in WinZip" in Chapter 5 for further information on how to fill in this box.

The three text boxes on the right of the dialog box refer to programs for compression of files in ARJ, LHA and ARC format. See the section on "Using other compression formats" in Chapter 5 for further information.

■ Other settings

If the Configuration dialog box is not displayed, use the **Configuration** command in the **Options** menu. Click on the **Miscellaneous** tab (see Figure 4.10).

The Miscellaneous tab contains the rest of the options that have not been defined under other tabs.

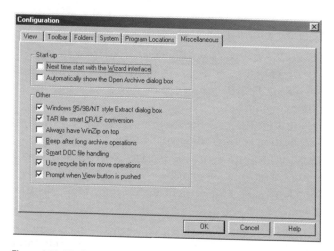

Figure 4.10 The Miscellaneous tab in the Configuration dialog box.

Start-up options

The **Start-up** option group determines the way in which WinZip will run when opened next. Choose the **Next time start with the Wizard interface** option, if you want to run in Wizard mode. Choose the **Automatically show the Open Archive dialog box** option if you want the **Open Archive** dialog box to be displayed automatically when opening WinZip.

Other options

The **Other** option group contains all the unclassified options:

- **Windows 95/98/NT style Extract dialog box.** This option determines the look of the Extract dialog box (see Figures 4.11 and 4.12)

- **TAR file smart CR/LF conversion.** Choose this option if you want to display text files in archives in TAR format created in Macintosh or UNIX. The Macintosh end of line characters CR (Carriage Return) and UNIX LF (Line

Figure 4.11 The Extract dialog box in Windows 3.1 style.

Feed) will be systematic-ally replaced with CR LF (stan-
dard on PC) so that the text is properly displayed

- **Always have WinZip on top.** When this option is chosen,
  the WinZip window is always in the foreground. This is
  practical if your screen is limited to a 640×480 pixel
  screen display

- **Beep after long archive operations.** Choose this option if
  you want to hear a beep every time WinZip completes a
  long compression operation (longer than one second)

- **Smart DOC file handling.** When this option is chosen,
  WinZip can detect whether a file with the **.DOC** extension

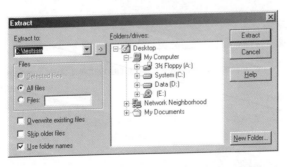

Figure 4.12 The Extract dialog box in the Windows 95/98/NT style.

contains simple text or if it is the product of text treatment. When you double-click on a file with the .DOC extension, this is displayed, after analysis, in the application associated to text files or in the application associated to .DOC files

- **Use recycle bin for move operations.** When you select the action **Move File** in the **Add** and **Drop** dialog boxes, the files affected may be placed in the recycle bin or definitely deleted according to the status of the option chosen

- **Prompt when View button is pushed.** When you select this option, the **View** dialog box is displayed when you click on the **View** button to display one of the files in an archive. You can also choose the viewing program associated with the type of file, an ASCII display built-in to WinZip or another program (see Figure 4.13). If this option is not chosen, the file is displayed with the program associated with its extension. If there are no programs associated with this file type, it will be displayed in the program whose name was specified in **Viewer**, under the **Program Locations** tab of the **Configuration** dialog box.

Figure 4.13 The View dialog box allows you to choose the display program.

5 Advanced use

Using other compression formats
Defining a self-extracting archive
Using an antivirus utility in WinZip
Protecting an archive with a password
Creating archives spanning several diskettes

This lesson deals with advanced techniques for WinZip. You will learn, among other things, to use other compression formats, to use an antivirus utility and to create archives spanning several diskettes.

■ Using other compression formats

The WinZip program comes with a compressor/decompressor for the ZIP format. It can also decompress files in **CAB**, **TAR**, **Z**, **GZ**, **TAZ**, **TGZ**, **UUencoded**, **Xxencoded**, **BinHex** and **MIME** format without the help of external programs. If you want to compress and/or decompress files in **ARJ**, **LHA** and **ARC** format with WinZip, you will need to use external compression/decompression programs:

- **LZH** files are created in the **LHA.EXE** program developed by Haruyasu Yoshizaki

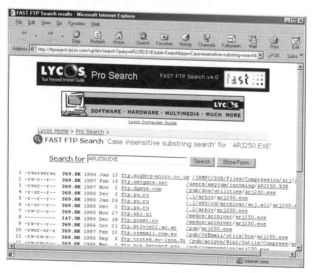

Figure 5.1 Searching for MS-DOS ARJ.EXE with FTPSearch.

- **ARJ** files are created in the **ARJ.EXE** program developed by Robert Yung

- Finally, **ARC** files are created in one of the following programs:

  - **ARCE.COM** or **ARC-E.COM** version 4.0e by Vern Berg

  - **PKXARC.EXE** version 3.6, 3.6 or 3.61 by PKWARE, Inc.

  - **ARC.EXE** version 5.20 or 6.0 by System Enhancement Associates, Inc.

You will easily be able to find these programs on the Internet with a Web search engine, an Archie site or FTPSearch. Some useful information:

- The **LHA.EXE** program is distributed as a self-extracting archive called **LHA213.EXE**

- The **ARJ.EXE** program is distributed as a self-extracting archive called **ARJ250.EXE** (see Figure 5.1)

- Finally, the **ARC.EXE**, **PKXARC.EXE** and **ARCE.EXE** programs can be found under these names.

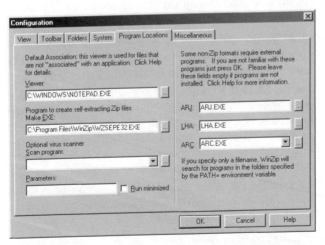

Figure 5.2 Compressed ARJ, LZH and ARC files can now be used in WinZip.

Once you have downloaded the required compression/
decompression programs, use the **Configuration** command in
the **Options** menu, select the **Program Locations** tab and
enter the path and the name of the programs you want to use
on the right-hand area of the dialog box (see Figure 5.2).

■ Defining a self-extracting archive

If you are used to sending compressed files either on diskettes,
or by Internet, to people who are not totally familiar with
compression/decompression software, a clever solution is to
send them a **self-extracting archive**.

Self-extracting archives come as executable programs. To
access the files they contain, you simply run the program.

WinZip includes a tool which allows to make a .ZIP archive
into a self-extracting file with just a few clicks. Let's see how
to do this with the help of an example. Let us suppose that
you want to change the **all.zip** file to become a self-extracting archive. This is what you do:

1. Click on the **Open** button in the WinZip window and
   open the **all.zip** file (you can also go through the **Favorites**
   folder to make things easier).

2. Use the **Make .EXE File** command in the **Actions** menu or
   press **Shift-K**. A dialog box will tell you that self-extracting archives generated by the shareware version of WinZip
   cannot be distributed (see Figure 5.3). If you want to use
   these archives for commercial purposes, you must first
   purchase the registered version of WinZip.

3. Click on the **OK** button and indicate the destination folder
   for the self-extracting archive, as well as the format of the
   generated file (see Figure 5.4).

The **Self Extracting Type** option group defines the storage
method for the files in the self-extracting archive:

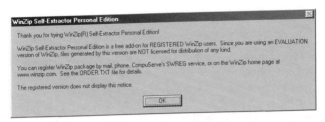

Figure 5.3 Self-extracting archives generated by WinZip cannot be used for commercial purposes.

- **16-bit Windows 3.1.** In this format, long filenames in the compressed folder will be truncated
- **32-bit Windows 95, 98, and NT.** In this format, long filenames will not be cut. On the other hand, the self-extracting archive will not be able to run in a 16-bit Windows 3.1 or 3.11 environment.

Ignore the **Spanning Support** option group if you are not intending to distribute the archive on diskette and/or the

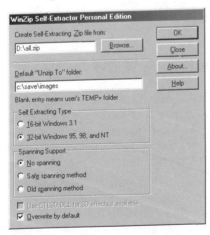

Figure 5.4 In this example, the self-extracting archive is in 32-bit format. It will be unzipped into the recipient's C:\save\images folder.

archive size is less than 1.44 Mb. If this is not so, you will need to select the method for splitting files on diskettes:

- **Safe spanning method.** Two files are placed on the first diskette: the first part of the archive and a small decompression program. The other diskettes will contain the following parts of the archive, in .ZIP format. This is the default storing method, which eliminates some problems that occurred with previous versions of WinZip

- **Old spanning method.** An executable file containing the first part of the archive and the decompression program is placed on the first diskette. The following diskettes contain the remaining parts of archive, stored in files with the .EXE extension. **Warning:** these files are not executable programs. If you try to open them from My Computer or from Windows Explorer, you will get an error message on screen. It may even crash your computer.

Self-extracting archives are always a little big bigger than the corresponding ZIP files, because they include the code for decompressing their contents.

■ Using an antivirus utility in WinZip

Computer viruses can spell disaster: they can cause anything, from the destruction of certain files to the complete reformatting of your hard disk! Some viruses are harmless. They may simply wish you a Merry Christmas or simulate a graphic breakdown... just for fun!

Whether they are dangerous or just silly, you certainly want to remove them from your system immediately. You should also test new programs before installing them to avoid the risk of infection. This is where WinZip comes into its own. By specifying the name of an anti-virus utility installed on your hard disk and defining the appropriate settings in

WinZip, you will be able to test compressed files and self-extracting archives before installing them.

When you install WinZip, it looks for the following antivirus utilities in the section **App Paths** of Windows 95/98 registration files: SCAN95.EXE, SCAN32.EXE, NAVW32.EXE, NAVW.EXE, WNAPVIR.EXE, NAV.EXE, CPAV.EXE, MSAV.EXE, WSCAN, SCAN.EXE, WFINDVIR, TBSCAN and **F-PROT**. If it finds one of these, WinZip automatically configures itself to be able to use it. Therefore if one of these antivirus utilities was installed prior to installing WinZip, WinZip will be able to use it. To ensure that this is so, use the **Configuration** command in the **Options** menu and select the **Program Locations** tab. If an antivirus utility was found, it will appear in the **Optional virus scanner Scan program** drop down list (see Figure 5.5).

If you installed the antivirus utility after installing WinZip, you will need to set up manually the **Optional virus scanner**

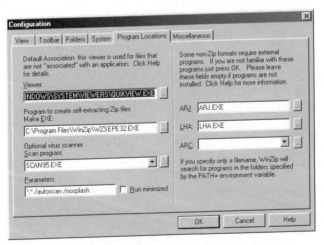

Figure 5.5 In this example, the McAfee SCAN32 antivirus utility has been identified and set up.

Scan program and Parameters controls in the Program Locations tab in the Configuration dialog box. Define the access path to the antivirus utility in the Optional virus scanner Scan program box and the parameters in the Parameters box. The following table provides the parameters needed for the most commonly used antivirus utilities.

Antivirus utility	Parameters
SCAN95.EXE	*.* /autoscan /nosplash
SCAN32.EXE	%d /autoscan /nosplash
NAVW32.EXE	*.* /s
NAVW.EXE	/auto *.* /S
WNAPVIR.EXE	/QM/M-/B- *.*
NAV.EXE	*.* /m- /s
CPAV.EXE	*.* /P
MSAV.EXE	*.* /P
WSCAN	%wscan
SCAN.EXE	/nomem *.* /ALL /SUB
WFINDVIR	%d
TBSCAN	*.* %d ln=%f lo nb nm
F-PROT	/NOBOOT /NOMEM /LIST *.* / REPORT=%f

The antivirus utility should now be available. This is how you use it:

1. Open the ZIP, ARJ, LZH, EXE self-extracting archive, or the file of the format to be tested by clicking on the Open button.

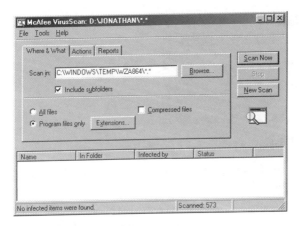

Figure 5.6 In this example, the ZIP archive tested by McAfee VirusScandoes not contain a virus.

2. Use the **Virus Scan** command in the -**Actions** menu or the keyboard shortcut **Shift-S**. This action decompresses the archive in a temporary folder and opens the antivirus utility window (see Figure 5.6).

■ Protecting an archive with a password

Archives that you send to a third party may well contain confidential information. If this is the case, you do not want anybody but the addressee to be able to access this confidential data. WinZip is able to associate a password with the compressed files and self-extracting archives it creates. This is how it is done:

1. Click on the **New** button to create a new ZIP file.
2. Enter the name of the new file and confirm.
3. Click on the **Password** button and define the password (see Figure 5.7).

89

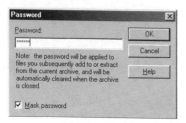

Figure 5.7 **Applying a password to a ZIP file.**

4. Select the files to be placed in the archive and click on the **Add** button.

The ZIP archive has now been created. The files included are protected by a password. Their names appear with a plus sign (+) in the WinZip window to indicate that they are password-protected (see Figure 5.8).

When the recipient wants to decompress the ZIP file, a dialog box will ask for the password. Decompression will not be carried out until the correct password is entered.

Name	Modified	Size	Ratio	Packed	Path
pkware newsgroup...	07/12/98 09...	194 450	83%	32 848	
pkware mailing list....	07/12/98 09...	230 708	82%	40 817	
winzip mailing list.ps...	07/12/98 09...	448 862	59%	181 941	
02-01.psp+	07/12/98 11...	182 045	60%	72 822	
01-01.psp+	07/12/98 11...	52 962	89%	5 815	
01-02.psp+	07/12/98 11...	63 659	89%	7 249	
01-03.psp+	07/12/98 11...	181 270	60%	72 510	
01-04.psp+	07/12/98 11...	190 792	61%	74 458	
01-05.psp+	07/12/98 11...	160 414	58%	67 857	
01-06.psp+	07/12/98 11...	152 023	57%	65 536	
01-07.psp+	07/12/98 11...	77 610	90%	7 615	

Selected 0 files, 0 bytes   Total 27 files, 3 889KB

Figure 5.8 **The files whose names are followed by a plus sign are password-protected.**

The recipient may have different decompression software. Even in this case, the password is required. This type of protection is therefore valid irrespective of the decompression software used.

Let us now suppose that you want to use the password-protection function to protect only some of the files in an archive. Follow these five steps:

1. Click on the **New** button to create a new ZIP file.

2. Enter the name of the new compressed file and confirm.

3. Add the files you do not need to be password-protected.

4. Use the **Password** command in the **Options** menu and define the password.

5. Click on the **Add** button and add the files to be protected by the password defined in Step 4.

The unprotected files can be unzipped by anyone with the appropriate decompression software. The protected files, on the other hand, can only be accessed using the correct password.

■ Creating archives spanning several diskettes

If you are sending ZIP files to a third party on diskettes, you may find that some archives cannot be placed on a single diskette. There are two possible solutions:

■ If the size of the ZIP files to be sent is very important, change the type of media. Use 100 MB **ZIP** disks, 1 GB **Jaz** or **Spark**, 1.5 GB **SyJet** and so on. In this case, the recipient of the files must obviously be able to read the media you are sending

■ If the ZIP files can be stored on a small number of diskettes, use WinZip **spanning**.

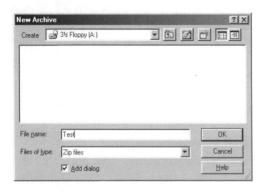

Figure 5.9 In this example, the Test.zip archive is created on the diskette drive A:.

To split a ZIP file over several diskettes, you must create it on a diskette rather than in the hard disk:

1. Click on the **New** button to create a new archive and define the archive name on a diskette (see Figure 5.9).

2. Specify the files to be included in the archive, insert an empty, formatted diskette in drive A: and confirm. When the first diskette is full, the dialog box shown in Figure 5.10 will appear.

3. Insert a new diskette, if necessary choose **Erase any existing files...** to delete any files that may be already stored on it and confirm. Repeat this operation until you have finished creating the ZIP file.

Figure 5.10 First diskette full. Insert new diskette.

ZIP files saved over several disks all have the same name. It is therefore very important that the diskettes should be carefully labelled and numbered for identification purposes.

To decompress a file which takes up several diskettes, insert the first diskette into the drive. View the contents and double-click on the ZIP file. The dialog box shown in Figure 5.11 is displayed.

Figure 5.11 WinZip prompts you to insert the last diskette.

Follow the instructions provided to restore the original files.

6 Browser extensions

An add-on, which can be freely downloaded from the WinZip Web site, significantly simplifies downloading files from the Net and on-line services. This module is compatible with most versions of Netscape Navigator/ Communicator and Internet Explorer. In this lesson, you will learn how to download it, install it and use it.

■ Downloading the add-on from the Internet

The WinZip Web site suggests using a supplementary module (add-on) for automating the process of sending files with a Web browser. Go to **http://www.winzip.com/ddchome.htm**. You will find a lot of useful information about this add-on (see Figure 6.1).

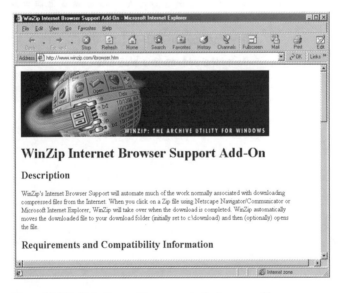

Figure 6.1 This Web site provides access to the browser add-on.

This complementary module has been tested successfully on the following browsers:

- Netscape Navigator 3.03 and 3.04
- Netscape Communicator 4.01a, 4.03, 4.04, 4.05, 4.06, 4.07, 4.08, 4.5 and 4.5 PR2
- Internet Explorer 3.02, 4.0, 4.01, 4.01 SP-1, 5Beta1 and 5Beta2.

Download the **WZINET95.EXE** file by clicking on the link **Download WinZip Internet Browser Support Add-On** and run it. The add-on is installed by default in the same folder as WinZip. A dialog box prompts you to copy automatically the downloaded files in the folder **c:\download** and to open them in WinZip after downloading. If necessary, modify one or both of the two default options (see Figure 6.2).

If you use a more recent version of the browsers listed above, check with a Web site which will confirm the compatibility of

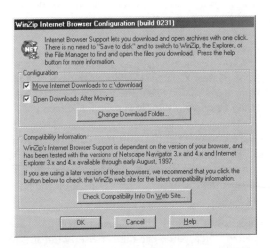

Figure 6.2 Configuration of the Internet browser add-on.

••

the add-on. Confirm your choice by clicking on the OK button. The supplementary module is now installed and is ready for use.

 *After installation of the add-on, you can still change the destination folder and/or stop WinZip from starting up after downloading. To do this, click on the **Start** button and select **Programs, WinZip**, then **Internet Browser Support Configuration**. Modifications are carried out in the dialog box that was displayed when the add-on was installed.*

■ Using the add-on in a web site

Go to a Web or ftp site and click on a link which represents a ZIP file. To download, you only need a single-click. The file is automatically placed in the **c:\download** folder. When you have finished downloading, the contents of the ZIP file is displayed in WinZip. With another click, the file is decompressed in the folder of your choice.

 *Several archives are distributed on the Net in a self-extracting format. The add-on for the Internet does not deal automatically with these types of files. You can therefore open them with the **Open** command in the WinZip **File** menu by right-clicking on the file and selecting **Open with WinZip** in the context menu.*

If you download a compressed file with Netscape Navigator/ Communicator or Internet Explorer without having first installed the Internet add-on, a dialog box offers you the choice between opening the archive and saving it on the hard disk (see Figure 6.3).

Warning. If you choose to open the archive rather than save it, it will be deleted when you close the browser window. To avoid this problem, use the **Save as** command in the **File** menu of the Explorer to save to a folder of your choice.

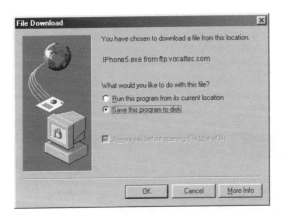

Figure 6.3 Choose between opening the archive and saving it to disk.

■ Problems with downloading

Sometimes, when you download, you are either un-successful or the outcome is a collection of corrupt files which cannot be opened in WinZip. This can be caused by a defective phone line, a busy or overloaded line, or maybe because either the receiving or the sending computer is overloaded. When WinZip gives you this type of message:

```
Cannot open file: it does not appear to be a valid
archive.
```

the best thing to do is start downloading again.

Occasionally, you may get an error message warning you that it one or more files cannot be downloaded. This means either that the file you are looking for is not at the address cross-referenced by the hypertext link or that the site which provided access to that file is too busy, or temporarily or permanently out of order. Wait for a few minutes, then try again...

■■

 *If the link to a file you want to download doesn't work, you may find the file on another site using the **FTPSearch** site. To do this, connect to **http://www.ftpsearch.ntnu.no/**, enter the name of the file you are looking for in the text box and confirm by pressing the **Enter** key on the keyboard. In a matter of seconds, one or more sites with the required file will be available (see Figure 6.4).*

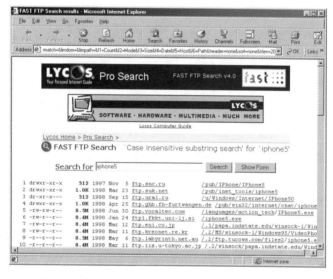

Figure 6.4 An example of a search in FTPSearch.

■ Some order wouldn't go amiss

And now, some practical advice if you download files regularly from the Internet.

First tip

Define two folders for downloading:

- **\DOWNLOAD** for downloading files
- **\ARCHIVES** for storing downloaded files you want to keep.

Second tip

Do not overcrowd the **\DOWNLOAD** and **\ARCHIVES** folders so that they become difficult to read. You should always define subfolders to classify files by origin or by subject.

Third tip

To get an idea of how useful an archive is and whether it suits your needs, do the following:

1. Double-click on the archive to open it in WinZip.

2. Read the documentation which comes with the archive. Most archives include a text file named **FILE_ID.DIZ** with a brief description. To view this file, double-click on it in the WinZip window. A message box will indicate that no viewing program has been associated to files with the .DIZ extension and will suggest using a default display. Confirm by clicking on the **Yes** button. The file opens in the Windows application **QuickView** (see Figure 6.5).

 If QuickView is not installed in your computer, proceed as follows:

*1. Display the Control panel (**Start** button then **Settings**, **Control panel**).*

*2. Double-click on the **Add/Remove programs** icon.*

*3. Click on **Accessories**, then click on the **Details** button.*

*4. Choose the **QuickView** option and confirm.*

QuickView is now operational. Simply call it up in the WinZip Program Locations dialog box.

3. Install the software contained in the archive. When an installation program named **INSTALL.EXE** or **SETUP.EXE**

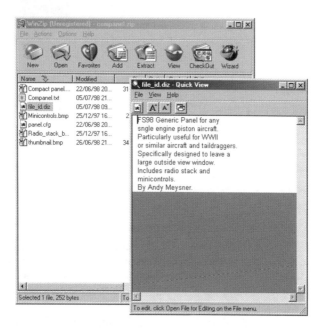

Figure 6.5 Displaying the FILE_ID.DIZ file in Windows QuickView.

is detected in the archive, the WinZip toolbar displays another button: **Install**. Simply click on this button to carry out the installation. Otherwise, you may click on the **CheckOut** button to copy the files into a specific folder and define a program group and icons in the **Start** menu (see Figure 6.6).

4. Use the **Folder** text box to specify the destination folder for the files in the archive, and the **Group name** text box to define the group name into which you want to place the icons for the installed elements (if you choose the **Create icons for programs and documents only** option, icons are created only for the program and the documents of that file type). You may want to choose the **Run virus scanner**

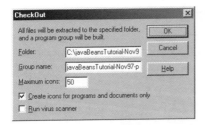

Figure 6.6 Installing an archive.

option if you want to run your antivirus utility to scan the application you are installing. When the installation is complete, the installed program and documents icons are available in **Programs/***group* of the **Start** menu (where *group* is the name of the group defined in the **CheckOut** dialog box).

5. If you like the software, move the archive to the **\ARCHIVES** folder to give some breathing space to the **\DOWNLOAD** folder, or else delete it to create some free space on your hard disk. If you do not like the software, uninstall it with the Windows un-installation program or with the one provided with the software, then delete the archive from the **\DOWNLOAD** folder.

 Several recent applications can be uninstalled with an uninstallation program supplied together with Windows 95/98. This is what you do:

*Click on the **Start** button and select **Settings**, then **Control panel** in the menu.*

*Double-click on the **Add/Remove program** icon in the Control panel. A list of applications that can be uninstalled appears in the central box of the list (see Figure 6.7).*

6. Click on the name of the application to be uninstalled in the list box, then on the **Add/Remove** button. Uninstallation occurs after confirmation.

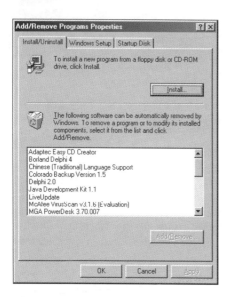

Figure 6.7 Uninstallation of an application.

Fourth tip

The Favorites concept is important in WinZip. It allows you to find the archives you need quickly. To go to **Favorites,** click on the **Favorites** icon in the toolbar, use the **Favorite Zip Folder** command in the **File** menu or the **Shift-F** keyboard shortcut. Whichever method you use, the ZIP files will be displayed in the **Favorite Zip Folders** dialog box (see Figure 6.8).

To complete the list, the easiest way is to click on the **Search** button to carry out a search on one or more drives (see Figure 6.9).

If your hard disk contains many ZIP files, you may want to limit the Favorites list. Click on the **Options** button, then on the **Add a folder to list** button to specify manually the folder

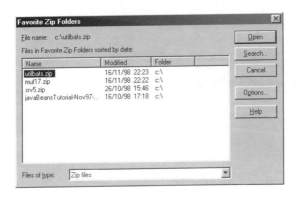

Figure 6.8 The Favorites window.

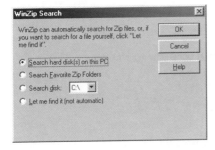

Figure 6.9 Global search for archives on one or more drives.

or folders which contain the ZIP files you want to examine
(see Figure 6.10).

Fifth tip

Never hesitate to get rid of archives you no longer need or
which are not relevant to you. Not only will you free your
hard disk but you will also improve the visibility of the folders you are keeping in your archives.

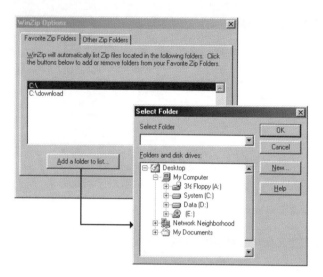

Figure 6.10 Manual selection of folders for examination.

7 WinZip tips

■ Starting WinZip more easily

If you are still not comfortable with the four methods of starting WinZip mentioned so far, you can use a keyboard shortcut for the WinZip shortcut icon. Whatever application you are in, you simply type the keyboard shortcut to access the WinZip window.

This is how to do it.

1. Right-click on the **Start** button.
2. Select **Open** in the menu. The WinZip shortcut icon is displayed in the window named **Start Menu** (see Figure 7.1).

Figure 7.1 The WinZip shortcut icon.

3. Right-click on the icon and select **Properties** in the menu. This action displays a dialog box named **WinZip properties** (see Figure 7.2).

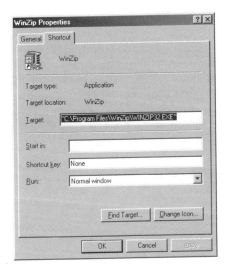

Figure 7.2 The WinZip properties window.

4. Click on the **Shortcut keys** text box and define a shortcut with the **Alt**, **Ctrl** and **Shift** keys containing a letter or a number, for example **Ctrl-Shift-W**. When you press the shortcut keys, they are automatically entered in the text box.

5. Confirm by clicking on the **OK** button.

Now you can start WinZip using the keyboard shortcut you have defined, regardless of which application is being run.

 *The keyboard shortcut can only function properly if it does not conflict with other keyboard shortcuts in the current application. For example, if you have set the keyboard shortcut **Shift-Ctrl-V** in WinZip, you will not be able to use the same shortcut in Paint Shop Pro. This keyboard shortcut in fact corresponds to the **Set Palette Transparency** command in the **Colors** menu in Paint Shop Pro.*

■ Adding a file to an existing archive

To add a file to an existing archive, click with the right mouse button in My Computer or in Explorer, and choose **Add to Zip** in the context menu. If an archive is open in WinZip, the file will be added to it, after confirmation (see Figure 7.3). Otherwise, a new archive with the same name as the file and with the **.ZIP** extension will be created, again after confirmation.

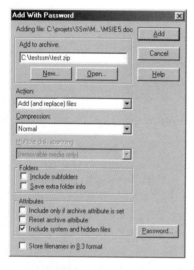

Figure 7.3 Adding a file in the current test.zip archive.

Alternatively, you can extract one or more files from WinZip and drag them and drop them into the folder of your choice in My Computer or in Explorer.

■ Viewing a file contained in an archive

To add a file contained in an archive, simply drag it from the WinZip window towards the icon of a suitable application. You can also right-click on the file in the WinZip window and select **Open** in the context menu. The file will be opened in the application to which it is linked.

If there is no application associated with this type of file, select **View** in the context menu and specify the application to be used in the text box of the **View** dialog box (see Figure 7.4).

Figure 7.4 Selecting an application to which you can add an archived file.

■ Printing a file contained in an archive

Following the same principles outlined above, you can print a file contained in an archive by dragging that file from the WinZip window and dropping it onto your printer shortcut. This will prove especially useful if you have shortcuts to your printers on the Windows desktop.

Otherwise, this is what you do:

1. Click on the **Start** button and select **Settings**, then **Printers**. This action displays a folder with all the printers available from your computer (see Figure 7.5).

Figure 7.5 List of installed printers.

2. Select the printer for which you want to create a shortcut on the Desktop. Keep the right mouse button pressed and place the printer icon in the Desktop. Select **Create short-cut(s) here** once you have released the mouse button.

■ Let's not lose sight of WinZip

Click with the right mouse button on the WinZip icon in the taskbar and select **Always on top** in the context menu so the WinZip window is always in the foreground.

■ Automatic decompression

Decompressing a .ZIP archive can be carried out even when WinZip is not running. Drag and drop the archive to be decompressed into a folder in My Computer or in Explorer. Right-click on the **.ZIP** file and select **Extract to folder** in the context menu.

■ Using favorites properly

If you store most of your archives in the same folder, it would be useful to define this folder as the default in WinZip. Use the **Configuration** command in the **Options** menu, select the **Folders** tab and define your preferred folder in the Folder text box of the **Start-up folder** option group (see Figure 7.6). In this way, when you create a new archive or you open an existing archive, the folder specified in this dialog box will be examined first.

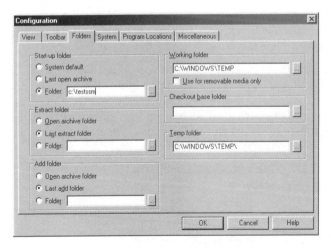

Figure 7.6 Defining a preferred start-up folder.

 The start-up folder will only become active after restarting WinZip.

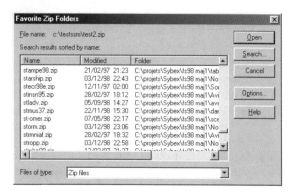

Figure 7.7 Favorites group the stored archives in some or all the folders in the system.

If you do not remember where your archives are stored, use the **Favorite Zip Folders** command in the **File** menu. To make life easier, the files kept as favorites can be classified by name, by date when last modified or by folder (see Figure 7.7).

For easier access to a file when you do not know its name, click on the **Name** field and type its initial. If the file you are searching for is not found, click on the **Search** button and specify the search method (see Figure 7.8). By selecting the **Search hard disk(s) on this PC** option, you will search all the archives on every drive in your computer.

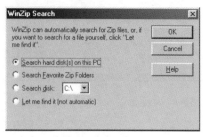

Figure 7.8 Updating Favorites.

■ Transferring files between two archives

You can copy or move files from one archive to another. To do this, you must open two WinZip windows and display the "source" and "destination" archives in each one. A simple drag and drop between the two WinZip windows is sufficient to copy/move. This action displays a dialog box named **Drag and Drop** (see Figure 7.9). Choose **Add (and replace) files** in the **Action** drop down list to copy the file to the destination archive. Choose **Move files** to move the file to the destination archive.

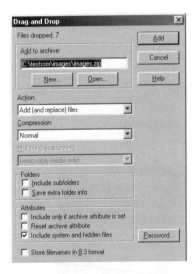

Figure 7.9 Copying or moving a file from one archive to another.

*If you cannot open two WinZip windows, open the **Options** menu and use the **Reuse WinZip Windows** command to deactivate the option chosen before this command.*

....

■ Reviewing ZIP files in your system

With a few clicks, WinZip can display a list of all the ZIP files in your system, on a drive or in a specific folder. To access this really helpful function, click on the **Favorites** buttons in the toolbar of WinZip in Classic mode. If this is the first time you have clicked the **Favorites** button after launching WinZip, the dialog box in Figure 7.10 is displayed.

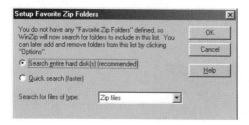

Figure 7.10 Selecting the search type.

If you select the **Search Entire Hard Disk(s)** option, the ZIP files are sought in all the folders in your system. If, on the

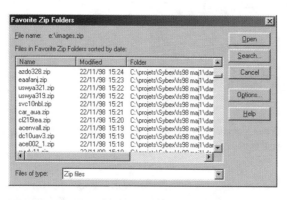

Figure 7.11 The list of ZIP files found.

other hand, you select the **Quick Search** option, the ZIP files are only sought in the **c:\cserve\download** and **c:\aol\download** folders. When the search is completed, the ZIP files which have been found appear in the dialog box shown in Figure 7.11. This dialog box will be displayed every time you click on the **Favorites** button.

The folders containing the displayed ZIP files are called "Favorites". If necessary, you can modify the list by clicking on the **Options** button in the **Favorite Zip Folders** dialog box. Click on the **Add a folder to list** button to add a new folder. Select a folder and click on the **Remove folder** button to delete it (see Figure 7.12).

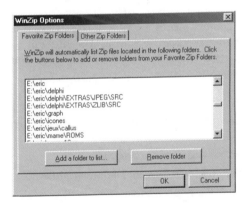

Figure 7.12 The list of Favorites can be modified.

WinZip does not just display the list of ZIP files in your system. By selecting one of the files displayed and clicking on the **Open** button, you can also open a ZIP file, for example, to add or delete files, or to decompress its contents into the folder of your choice.

■ Viewing the contents of files in an archive without decompressing it

Windows 95 and 98 both have an extremely helpful document-viewing tool: **QuickView**. If it is installed, you can use it to display some types of files stored in a compressed archive, without having to decompress it. To do this, use the **Configuration** command in the **Options** menu. Select the **Program Locations** tab, type the word **quickview** in the **Viewer** text box and confirm. The word "quickview" is replaced by the complete path of the **QuickView.exe** program, namely as **c:\WINDOWS\SYSTEM\VIEWERS\ QUIKVIEW.EXE**. To view a file which appears in the WinZip window, click on it with the right mouse button and select **View** in the context menu. A dialog box will propose the associated viewing program. Confirm. The file will be displayed in the corresponding QuickView program, without having to decompress the archive.

 If QuickView is not installed in your computer, do the following:

*1. Call up the Control panel (**Start** button then **Settings** and **Control panel**).*

*2. Double-click on the **Add/Remove programs** icon.*

*3. Click on **Accessories**, then click on the **Details** button.*

*4. Choose the **QuickView** option and confirm.*

QuickView is now functional. You only need to define it in the **WinZip Program Locations** dialog box.

8
The WZunzip program

The **Wzunzip.exe** program is used to decompress **.ZIP** files created with WinZip or with other compression software. It is a very comprehensive program and its commands are often complex enough to put off new users. But with a little practice, you realise that WZunzip is not only extremely powerful, but also fairly easy to use.

■ Running WZunzip

The WZunzip program can be run:

■ in an MS-DOS window

■ in the Run dialog box

■ in a batch command file.

Let's examine these three possibilities.

MS-DOS Window

Click on the **Start** button and select **Programs/MS-DOS Prompt.** The window shown in Figure 8.1 is displayed.

Figure 8.1 The MS-DOS Prompt window.

Figure 8.2 Using WZunzip in an MS-DOS window.

Now simply go to the folder containing the file or files to be decompressed (with the MS-DOS CD command) and use the **WZunzip** command (see Figure 8.2).

This command assumes that:

1. The folder containing the **TEST** archive is the active folder.
2. The WinZip installation folder has been defined in the **PATH** settings of the **AUTOEXEC.BAT** file.

To be sure that the second condition is fulfilled, display the root of drive C: in My Computer or in Windows Explorer. Find the **AUTOEXEC.BAT** file icon. Click on this icon with the right mouse button and select **Edit** in the context menu. The following lines are an example of the **AUTOEXEC.BAT** file:

```
C:\PROGRA~1\NETWOR~1\MCAFEE~1\SCANPM.EXE C:\
@IF ERRORLEVEL 1 PAUSE
mode con codepage prepare=((850)
C:\WINDOWS\COMMAND\ega.cpi)
mode con codepage select=850
keyb uk,,C:\WINDOWS\COMMAND\keyboard.sys
set path= c:\utils;c:\windows\command;
```

In this example, the **PATH** settings do not refer to the WinZip application. We are going to modify this line as follows:

```
set path= c:\utils;c:\windows\command;
c:\progra~1\winzip
```

After restarting your computer, the executable files in the **c:\Program Files\WinZip** folder (and specifically **Wzzip.exe** and **Wzunzip.exe**) can be run directly from any folder.

 If the name of the file to be decompressed includes one or more spaces, it must be enclosed in quotation marks, for example:
```
Wzunzip"Winzip in a day.zip"
```

The Run dialog box

Click on the **Start** button and select **Run** in the menu. This action displays the **Run** dialog box (see Figure 8.3).

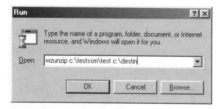

Figure 8.3 The Run dialog box.

Type the WZunzip command in the text box of the **Run** window, specifying the complete path of the file to be decompressed and the destination path of the resulting files.

 You can use the –YP parameter to prevent the MS-DOS command window from closing immediately after decompression. Type, for example, a command of the following type:
```
Wzunzip -yp c:\testssm\test c:\destin
```

In this way you can check out the information in the MS-DOS window. Simply press the Enter key on the keyboard to close this window.

Batch command file

Batch command files are text files containing one or more **MS-DOS** commands. They are used to automate some tasks, such as daily saving of a folder, compression of an archive and its storage on a different disk drive or even the execution of a program to which you send files within a given folder on a regular basis. The **WZunzip** command can also be used in a **batch** file to automate some decompression, but do be careful, the batch file must be run under Windows 95/98/NT. In fact, the WZunzip command is not compatible with pure MS-DOS mode.

Example:

This is the **batch** file which lists the contents of the **d:\saved.zip** archive and copies its contents to the current folder on drive **c:**, restoring its tree structure.

```
Wzunzip -v d:\saved.zip >prn:
Wzunzip -d d:\saved.zip c:\current
```

To define a **batch** file, you will use Windows Notepad (remember that the **Programs/Accessories/Notepad** command in the **Start** menu launches this utility). Enter the command lines and save the file giving it the **.bat** extension.

To run this **batch** file, simply double-click on it in My Computer or in Windows Explorer.

■ Using the WZunzip program

First, we will describe the most useful parameters in the WZunzip program.

Parameter	Function
–D	Restores the tree structure of the files stored in the archive
–N	Extracts only new files created after the original files
–O	Overwrites existing files with the same name
–T	Tests the integrity of the ZIP file
–V	Displays the contents of the archive
–X	Excludes one or more files from the extraction process
–S	Uses a password for decompression

The following pages specify how to use these parameters on the basis of examples.

■ Basic use

The most common way of using WZunzip is to specify only the name of the archive to be decompressed. For example:

```
Wzunzip TEST
```

The files contained in the TEST archive have been decompressed and saved in the current folder. If there are one or more files with the same name, you will see a message asking you whether the old files should be overwritten by the new ones or if they should be preserved. For example:

```
Eiffel Tower.bmp exists. Overwrite ([y]es, [n]o,
[a]ll, q[uit])?
```

Choose **Y** (Yes) to overwrite the old file, **N** (No) to keep it, **A** (All) to overwrite all the files with the same name or **Q** (Quit) to exit WZunzip.

■ Restoring an archive tree structure

As you already know, WinZip can create an archive by saving the exact contents of a folder, even if this contains one or more subfolders. To restore its exact tree structure to an archive, use the **–d** parameter.

By way of an example, the following command decompresses the **data.zip** archive (in the current folder) in the folder **c:\destin**, restoring the original tree structure:

```
Wzunzip -D DATA.ZIP C:\DESTIN
```

If the **C:\DESTIN** folder does not exist, it is created by WZunzip. If the archive does not contain any tree structure information, the **–d** parameter is simply ignored.

Overwrite or update existing files

By adding the **–O** parameter to a WZunzip command, the decompressed files overwrite any files with the same name present in the destination folder:

```
Wzunzip -O DATA.ZIP C:\DESTIN
```

On the other hand, by adding the **–N** parameter, only the files with the same name but with an earlier creation or modification date than those in the archive are overwritten:

```
Wzunzip -n DATA.ZIP C:\DESTIN
```

■ Testing the integrity of an archive

You have just received an archive named TEST.ZIP. To test its integrity, use the following command:

```
Wzunzip -T A:\TEST.ZIP
```

This command specifies that the archive is stored on the diskette in drive A:.

All the files in the archive are subject to an integrity test. Their names are displayed on screen followed by the **OK** label or by an error message. This is an example of the feedback provided by WZunzip:

```
C:\testssm>Wzunzip -t test
WinZip(R) 7.0X beta (1301) Command Line Interface
Copyright (c) Nico Mak Computing, Inc. 1991-1998
- All Rights Reserved

Zip file: test.zip
    testing: WinZip in a day.doc    OK
    testing: images/                    OK
    testing: images/pkware newsgroups.psp    OK
    testing: images/pkware mailing list.psp    OK
    testing: images/winzip mailing list.psp    OK
    testing: images/02-01.psp          OK
    testing: images/01-01.psp          OK
    testing: images/01-02.psp          OK
    testing: images/01-02.psp          OK
    testing: images/01-03.psp          OK
    testing: images/01-04.psp          OK
    testing: images/01-05.psp          OK
    testing: images/01-06.psp          OK
    testing: images/01-07.psp          OK
    testing: images/01-08.psp          OK
    testing: images/01-09.psp          OK
    testing: images/01-11.psp          OK
    testing: images/01-10.gif          OK
    testing: images/01-12.psp          OK
```

```
testing: images/02-02.psp          OK
testing: images/02-03.psp          OK
testing: images/02-04.psp          OK
testing: images/02-05.psp          OK
testing: images/02-06.psp          OK
testing: images/02-07.psp          OK
testing: images/02-08.psp          OK
testing: images/02-09.psp          OK
testing: images/02-10.psp          OK
testing: images/02-11.psp          OK
testing: images/03-01.psp          OK
No errors detected in compressed data of test.zip.

C:\testssm>
```

In this example, all files are valid.

Some archives contain a large number of files. When you test the integrity of these archives, you may miss some error messages, because the screen scrolls through them very quickly. You have two solutions.

First solution

You may stop the scrolling when the screen is full by adding the |MORE command to the command.

For example:

```
Wzunzip -T A:\TEST.ZIP |MORE
```

Second solution

You may direct the display to a text file to be examined at leisure.

Type for example:

```
Wzunzip -T A:\TEST.ZIP >RESULT.TXT
```

In this example, information usually shown on screen is in fact stored in the **RESULT.TXT** text file.

If you attempt to test the integrity of an archive whose files are password-protected with a command similar to those we have just seen, you will get error message such as:

```
skipping pkware newsgroups.psp -- the file is
encrypted and its password wasn't specified
```

To solve this problem, add the −S parameter. For example:

```
Wzunzip -T -Spassword A:\TEST.ZIP
```

If you do not enter the password in the command (this may in practice not be convenient because the password is shown for all to see), you will be prompted for it just before decompression. In order to preserve the confidentiality of the password, the characters keyed in on the keyboard are replaced by asterisks on the screen. Naturally, the integrity test will only be carried out if the correct password is entered.

■ Displaying the contents of an archive

You have just downloaded a ZIP file. You may however not be interested in all the files included. To view its contents on screen, you need to use the –V parameter.

Type for example the following command to display the contents of the TEST.ZIP archive:

```
Wzunzip -V A:\TEST.ZIP
```

A sample printout of the feedback provided by WZunzip is shown the next page.

For each file you see:

- the actual length: **Length**
- the compression method: **Method**
- the size after compression: **Size**
- the reduction ratio: **Ratio**

```
WinZip(R) 7.0X beta (1301) Command Line Interface
Copyright (c) NicoMak Computing, Inc. 1991-1998 - All Rights Reserved

Zipfiletest.zip

Length  Method   Size  Ratio  Date       Time   CRC-32   Attr  Name
------  ------   ----  -----  ----       ----   ------   ----  ----
140288  DeflatN  38541  73%  07/12/1998  14:03  9bab494e --w-  WinZip en un jour.doc
     0  Stored       0   0%  07/12/1998  15:36  00000000 --wD  images/
194450  DeflatN  32836  84%  07/12/1998  09:27  18de765b --w-  images/pkware newsgroups.psp
230708  DeflatN  40805  83%  07/12/1998  09:27  3e6d7831 --w-  images/pkware mailing list.psp
448862  DeflatN 181929  60%  07/12/1998  09:27  e6fd347f --w-  images/winzip mailing list.psp
182045  DeflatN  72810  61%  07/12/1998  11:12  47453210 --w-  images/02-01.psp
 52962  DeflatN   5803  90%  07/12/1998  11:17  161b9530 --w-  images/01-01.psp
 63659  DeflatN   7237  89%  07/12/1998  11:18  eeafdab9 --w-  images/01-02.psp
181270  DeflatN  72498  61%  07/12/1998  11:18  843c2192 --w-  images/01-03.psp
190792  DeflatN  74446  61%  07/12/1998  11:19  a41630ea --w-  images/01-04.psp
160414  DeflatN  67845  58%  07/12/1998  11:21  976ce33e --w-  images/01-05.psp
152023  DeflatN  65524  57%  07/12/1998  11:28  322eba8d --w-  images/01-06.psp
 77610  DeflatN   7603  91%  07/12/1998  11:27  c8df9ea0 --w-  images/01-07.psp
156274  DeflatN  66416  58%  07/12/1998  11:30  40d7aa20 --w-  images/01-08.psp
168319  DeflatN  69203  59%  07/12/1998  11:31  fc8da6a7 --w-  images/01-09.psp
173740  DeflatN  69789  60%  07/12/1998  13:00  f70e7236 --w-  images/01-11.psp
  5427  DeflatN   4719  14%  25/02/1998  15:37  8266a93a --w-  images/01-10.gif
 98132  DeflatN  11861  88%  07/12/1998  13:05  26022d57 --w-  images/01-12.psp
227872  DeflatN  77867  66%  07/12/1998  13:42  e2532840 --w-  images/02-02.psp
160738  DeflatN  68263  58%  07/12/1998  13:43  e9413d06 --w-  images/02-03.psp
 87332  DeflatN   9148  90%  07/12/1998  13:44  4d67231e --w-  images/02-04.psp
173972  DeflatN  70678  60%  07/12/1998  13:54  0765333d --w-  images/02-05.psp
 98850  DeflatN  10954  89%  07/12/1998  13:55  fb98af8e --w-  images/02-06.psp
164363  DeflatN  68158  59%  07/12/1998  13:55  3a3f3ecc --w-  images/02-07.psp
130659  DeflatN  17288  87%  07/12/1998  13:57  565bb310 --w-  images/02-08.psp
101450  DeflatN  11429  89%  07/12/1998  13:57  72142f29 --w-  images/02-09.psp
118829  DeflatN  14492  88%  07/12/1998  14:02  500bf433 --w-  images/02-10.psp
 71272  DeflatN   7332  90%  07/12/1998  14:02  f1a12b18 --w-  images/02-11.psp
110255  DeflatN  26680  76%  07/12/1998  15:33  f107f62d --w-  images/03-01.psp
-------          -------  ----                                 ----
4122567         1272154  70%                                  29
```

- the date and time of creation of the compressed file: **Date and Time**

- the CRC value calculated in the CRC 32: **CRC-32 checking routine**

- the file attributes (read only, archive, hidden file, system file): **Attr**

- the filename: **Name**.

If you scroll through the contents of an archive with a large number of files, you are unlikely to be able to see all the information you need because of the fast scrolling of the screen.

You may stop the display when the screen is full by adding **M** to the **–V** parameter. For example:

```
Wzunzip -VM A:\TEST.ZIP
```

You may also direct the display to a text file to be examined at leisure. Type for example:

```
Wzunzip -V A:\TEST.ZIP >RESULT.TXT
```

In this example, information usually shown on screen is in fact stored in the **RESULT.TXT** text file.

The **–V** parameter can be terminated with a letter to define the order of display of the files:

Parameter	Type of sort
C	CRC
D	Date
E	Extension
N	Name

Parameter	Type of sort
O	Origination order
P	Compression percentage
S	Original size

For example, the following command displays the files in the TEST.ZIP archive, sorting them in alphabetical order:

```
Wzunzip -VN TEST.ZIP
```

If you want, you can invert the display order by adding the letter **R** to the –**V** parameter. For example, the following command displays the files in the **TEST.ZIP** archive, sorting them in reverse order of size (largest first, smallest last):

```
Wzunzip -VSR TEST.ZIP
```

■ Decompressing with exclusion of files

The –**X** parameter allows you to exclude one or more files from decompression of a ZIP file. For example, to de-compress all the files in the TEST.ZIP archive, apart from the files with the .SS extension and the SLICKS.DAT file, use the following command:

```
Wzunzip -X*.SS XSLICKS.DAT TEST
```

 There must not be a space between the –X parameter and the name of the file or the type of files to be excluded.

Partial decompression

For partial decompression of an archive, simply indicate the names of the files for extraction, if necessary with one or

more wildcards. Therefore, to extract all the files with the
.DOC extension and the **SLICKS.DAT** file from the
TEST.ZIP archive, type:

```
Wzunzip TEST *.DOC SLICKS.DAT
```

In this example, the selected files are placed in the folder
which includes the archive. If you want to transfer them to a
different folder, simply indicate this in the command:

```
Wzunzip TEST *.DOC SLICKS.DAT C:\DESTIN
```

■ Decompressing a password-protected archive

If you are attempting to decompress a password-protected
archive without providing the password, you will get an error
message for each protected file:

```
C:\testssm>Wzunzip password
WinZip(R) 7.0X beta (1301) Command Line Interface
Copyright (c) Nico Mak Computing, Inc. 1991-1998 - All
Rights Reserved

Zip file: password.zip

    skipping ./file_id.diz -- the file is
    -encrypted and its password wasn't specified
    skipping ./ReadMe.Txt -- the file is encrypted
    -and its password wasn't specified
    skipping ./sample.exe -- the file is encrypted
    -and its password wasn't specified

C:\testssm>
```

To decompress the archive, use a command of the following
type:

```
Wzunzip -Spassword Archive
```

where *password* is the password specified by the person who created the archive and *Archive* is the name of the archive to be decompressed.

We have not examined all the parameters of the WZunzip command. To obtain a full overview of the program, click on the **Start** button and select **Programs, WinZip,** then **Command Line Support Add-On Documentation.** The full list of WZunzip parameters can be found under the heading **Wzunzip Command Reference** (see Figure 8.4).

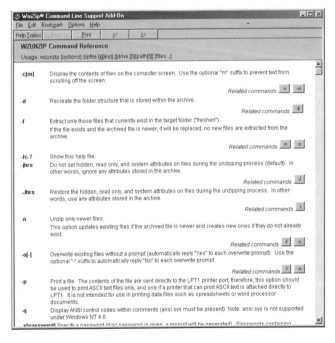

Figure 8.4 The WZunzip command parameters.

9 The WZzip program

The **Wzzip.exe** program is used to compress files in an archive in the WinZip format, using a command line. It is very exhaustive and powerful for specific cases, such as automatic daily compression of a folder before storing it or systematic compression of space-hungry media (video, sound and so on) just after their creation. If you are tempted, scroll through...

■ Running WZzip

The **Wzzip.exe** program is used to create new compressed archives in the WinZip format, and to update existing archives. Its command line is even more scary than its little brother **Wzunzip.exe**. But we will see that with a little practice WZzip is not as difficult to handle as it may appear at first.

Just like WZunzip, the WZzip program can be run:

- in an MS-DOS window
- in the Run dialog box
- in a batch command file.

Let us examine these three possibilities.

MS-DOS Window

Click on the **Start** button and select **Programs**, then **MS-DOS Prompt**. Simply go to the folder containing the file or files to be compressed (with the MS-DOS **CD** command) and use the **WZzip** command (see Figure 9.1).

This command assumes:

1. That the folder containing the TEST archive is the active folder.

Figure 9.1 An example of how to use WZzip in an MS-DOS window.

2. That the WinZip installation folder was saved in the
   PATH settings of the **AUTOEXEC.BAT** file.

Check the section on "The WZunzip program" in Chapter 8
for further information.

The Run dialog box

Click on the **Start** button and select **Run** in the menu. This
action displays the **Run** dialog box (see Figure 9.2).

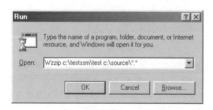

Figure 9.2 The Run dialog box.

Enter the wzzip command in the text box of the Run window, specifying the complete path for the files to be compressed and for the resulting archive.

You can use the –YP parameter to stop the MS-DOS command window from closing immediately after decompression. You could, for example type the following command:

```
Wzzip yp c:\testssm\test c:\source\*.*
```

*You will now be able to scroll through the information in the MS-DOS window. Simply press the **Enter** key on the keyboard to close this window.*

Batch command file

As previously mentioned, the batch command files automate repetitive operations. By inserting one or more **WZzip** commands in a batch file, you can quickly create archives which would have taken several minutes with WinZip.

Example:

In the following example the batch file creates an archive called **c:\testssm\test.zip** and stores in it all the files from the **c:\source** folder. Then it creates an archive called **c:\testssm\text.zip** and stores in it all the files with the **.doc** or **.txt** extensions from the **c:\documents** folder.

```
Wzzip -yp c:\testssm\test c:\source\*.*
Wzzip -yp c:\testssm\text c:\documents\*.doc
➡*.txt
```

*You can use the –YP parameter to avoid the MS-DOS command window closing as soon as the archive has been compressed. The **WZunzip** command can also be used in a batch file to automate several decompression tasks. But be careful, the batch file must be run under Windows 95/98/NT. The WZunzip command is in fact incompatible with MS-DOS.*

■ Using the WZzip program

Just as with **Wzunzip.exe**, we will only describe the most useful parameters for this program.

Parameter	Function
–A	Adds files to the archive
–D	Removes files from the archive
–U	Overwrites files with the latest versions
–P	Saves the file path
–R	Includes subfolders in the compression
–S	Defines a password
–V	Displays the contents of the archive
–&	Stores the archive on several volumes

The following pages will show you how to use these parameters with the help of examples.

■ Basic use

The most common way of using WZzip is to specify the name of the archive to be compressed. For example:

```
Wzzip TEST
```

This command compresses all the files in the current folder (but not in the subfolders). The archive is named **TEST.ZIP**.

If only some of the files are to be placed in the archive, simply specify their names after the archive name.

For example, the following command compresses the **TOTAL1.DOC** and **TOTAL2.DOC** files (in the current folder) and creates the **TEST.ZIP** archive:

```
Wzzip TEST TOTAL1.DOC TOTAL2.DOC
```

You can also use one or more wildcards to specify the name of the files to be compressed.

For example, the following command creates a compressed file named **TEST.ZIP**. Only files with six characters where the first two are **SL** and the last three are **CKS** are compressed. The file extension (.*) is ignored.

```
Wzzip TEST SL?CKS.*
```

To complete this description of the basic use of WZzip, remember that the files to be compressed do not all need to be in the same folder and that the resulting archive may be saved on a different drive or in a different folder from the one you are in.

For example, the command shown below instructs WZzip to create an archive called **TEST.ZIP** on the diskette in drive **A:** and to compress the following files:

- all files with the .DOC extension in the **Document** folder in drive **D:**
- all the files with the .GIF extension in the **Image** folder in drive **E:**.

```
Wzzip A:\TEST D:\DOCUMENT E:\IMAGE\*.GIF
```

If the name of the file to be compressed or of the archive contains one or more spaces, it must be enclosed in double quotes, such as:

```
Wzzip "Winzip in a day" "Winzip in a day.doc"
```

*This command compresses the **Winzip in a day.doc** document. The name of the compressed archive will be **Winzip in a day.zip**.*

■ Adding and removing files from an archive

WZzip can add files to and remove files from an existing archive. To do this, simply use the –A and –D parameters respectively.

As an example, this first command adds all the files in the current folder that have the .DOC extension to the T.ZIP archive, also in the current folder:

```
Wzzip -A T *.DOC
```

This second command removes all the files with the .DOC extension from the T.ZIP archive which is in the C:\TEST folder.

```
Wzzip -D C:\TEST\T.ZIP *.DOC
```

■ Updating files in an archive

The –U parameter allows you to update the files contained in an archive. It will only handle:

■ the files with a later creation date and time than the specified uncompressed files

■ the specified files which are not present in the archive.

As an example, this is the command to update the files with the .DOC extension in the T.ZIP archive:

```
Wzzip U T *.DOC
```

WZzip displays the following type of information:

```
updating WinZip in a day.doc
updating 01-10.gif
adding readme.txt
updating Zip file c:\testssm\test.zip
```

In this example, the **WinZip in a day.doc** and **01-10.gif** files have been updated and the **readme.txt** file has been added to the **test.zip** archive.

■ Compressing folders and subfolders

In some cases, you may want to create compressed files containing an entire folder. If the folder only contains files, simply call it up and type in the following command:

```
Wzzip DESTIN
```

All the files in the current folder will be copied to the **DESTIN.ZIP** archive.

On the other hand, if the folder contains one or more subfolders which also need to be included in the archive, you will need to use the **–RP** parameter:

```
Wzzip -RP DESTIN
```

The files, as well as the tree structure of the subfolders will be saved in the DESTIN.ZIP archive.

To restore the original data, use the **–D** parameter in the WZunzip command:

```
Wzunzip -D DESTIN
```

■ Protecting an archive with a password

If you need to send out archives which contain confidential information, you will want to protect the data. WZzip can attach a password to an archive. To decompress a password-protected archive, the recipient must know the password. Otherwise, whatever decompression program is used, the user will not be able to extract the files from the archive. To attach a password to an archive, use the –S parameter.

For example, the following command creates the password custom for the **RAL.ZIP** archive:

```
Wzzip -Scustom RAL
```

If the **RAL.ZIP** archive exists, it will be protected with the password **custom**. If it does not exist, it will be created and will be given the password **custom**.

To decompress a password-protected archive, use the following command:

```
Wzunzip -Spassword Archive
```

Where *password* is the password and *Archive* is the name of the archive to be decompressed.

Check the section on "Decompressing a password-protected archive" in Chapter 8 for further information on the subject.

■ Creating an archive spanning several volumes

If you want to copy an archive of several megabytes onto a diskette, you use a special command when creating it.

Let us suppose that you have the empty diskettes, ready and formatted. To compress the entire current folder over several diskettes, type the following command (the compressed **TEST.ZIP** file will be split over as many diskettes as necessary):

```
Wzzip -& A:\TEST
```

If your diskettes are formatted, but contain data, type this command:

```
Wzzip -&w A:\TEST
```

This command carries out a fast formatting of the diskettes before storing the archive.

To restore the original files in the **C:\DESTIN** folder, the final user must enter the two following commands:

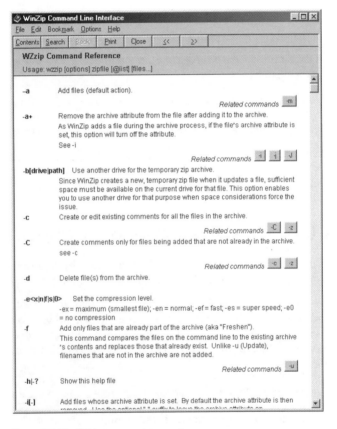

Figure 9.3 The WZzip command parameters.

```
A:
Wzunzip TEST.ZIP C:\DESTIN
```

Several messages will prompt you to insert the various diskettes which store the archive. **Warning:** it is absolutely vital that each diskette is carefully labelled and numbered when it is created. It is practically impossible to recognise them after creation, because the name of the archive will be the same on each diskette.

 *The **Wzzip –&** parameter can obviously be used for other types of removable media, such as Zip disks or SyQuest.*

We have not examined all of the WZzip parameters. For an exhaustive overview, click on the **Start** button and select **Programs, WinZip,** then **Command Line Support Add-On Documentation.** The complete list of WZzip parameters can be found under the heading **Wzzip Command Reference** (see Figure 9.3).

Part II

The Windows PKWare pack

■ ■ ■ ■ ■ ■ ■ ■ ■ ■ ■ ■ ■ ■ ■ ■ ■ ■ ■ ■

If you have been working with computers for some time, you may have come across the compression program which was all the rage in the early- to mid-90s: PKZip for MS-DOS. This program used to work with a command line which was certainly efficient but it was also something of a headache. PKWare, the company that developed the program, had the good sense to produce a Windows version. Less comprehensive than WinZip, but easier to use, it is impossible not to mention it in this book. Go through the next three lessons. You will then be able to make an informed choice as to the compression program which is best suited to your needs: WinZip or PKZip.

10

Before you begin

This lesson includes all the basic information necessary for starting to use the PKZip application for Windows. You will then learn how to install the program, uninstall it and start it.

■ The main features of PKZip

These are some of the main features of the PKZip application:

- **Supports long filenames.** Archives compressed with PKZip do not cut the long filenames used in Windows 95/98.

- **Supports a variety of compressed file formats.** PKZip supports the ZIP format. It is therefore possible to create compressed archives in ZIP format and unzip files contained in a ZIP archive. But PKZip does more than that: it can extract files saved in several other compression formats: **UUE** (*UUEncode*) **XXE** (*XXEncode*), **HQX** (*BinHex*), **MIM** and **MME** (*MIME*), **TAR** (*tar*), **GZ** and **TGZ** (*GZIP*).

- **Creates self-extracting compressed archives.** PKZip can create self-extracting archives. This type of archive is the preferred option if the recipient does not have the appropriate decompression software.

- **Runs .EXE files contained in .ZIP archives without having to decompress the archive.** When an archive contains an executable program, it can be launched without having to decompress the archive.

■ Installing the PKZip pack for windows

To install PKZip for Windows, follow these steps.

1. Download the self-extracting archive **PK260W32.EXE** (see the section "Downloading the latest version of PKZip" in this chapter).

2. View the folder in which you have stored the archive, in My Computer or Explorer, for example.

3. Double-click on **PK260W32.EXE**. The dialog box shown in Figure 10.1 is displayed. Select the drive and the installation folder, then click on the **Extract** button.

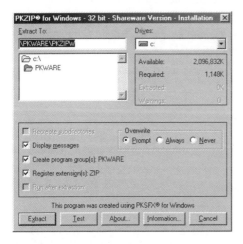

Figure 10.1 The PKZip for Windows installation dialog box.

Within a few seconds, PKZip for Windows is installed and ready to run. The PKWare suite of programs provides access to all the files in the application:

- **PKZip for Windows.** Double-click on this icon (or use the **Programs/PKWare/PKZip for Windows** command in the **Start** menu) to launch the PKZip application.

- **Read Me.** This file contains various details about the PKZip application: version, Web site, help, files used by the application, and so on.

- **PKZip for Windows Help.** PKZip on-line help. It is also available with the Index command in PKZip Help menu.

- **Order Form.** Information on how to register your copy of PKZip.

- **Go Online!.** Local Web page, for easy access to the PKZip registration site and for sending emails requesting technical support (this Web page can also be accessed with the **Go Online** command in the PKZip **Help** menu).

- **Uninstall.** PKZip uninstallation program (this program is also available with the **Programs/PKWare/Uninstall** command in the **Start** menu).

- **What's New.** List of what's new in PKZip version 2.60.

■ Starting PKZip

To launch PKZip for Windows, you have a number of options. You may:

1. Use the **Start** menu.
2. Create a shortcut icon on the Windows desktop and double-click on this icon.
3. Apply a keyboard shortcut to the **PKZip for Windows** icon of the **PKWare** suite of programs.
4. Double-click on an archive in ZIP format, in My Computer, Explorer or any other Windows file manager.

 If WinZip (or any other compression/decompression program) is associated to the .ZIP extension, a dialog box is displayed when

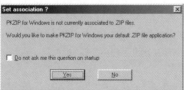

Figure 10.2 Changing the existing association.

*launching PKZip (see Figure 10.2). Click on the **Yes** button if you want to associate the ZIP extension to PKZip. If not, click on the **No** button. In the latter case, you can choose the option **Do not ask me this question on startup** if you do not want to have this dialog box displayed every time you start PKZip.*

With the Start menu

Click on the **Start** button then select **Programs**, **PKWare** and **PKZip for Windows**.

With a shortcut icon

Right-click on the **Start** button and select **Open** in the menu. A window named **Start-up menu** is displayed on screen. Double-click on the **Programs** icon, then on the **PKWare** icon. The previous window now has all the icons of PKZip for Windows. Select the **PKZip for Windows** icon. Keep the right mouse button pressed and place the icon on the desktop. Release the button and select **Create shortcut(s) here** in the context menu (see Figure 10.3).

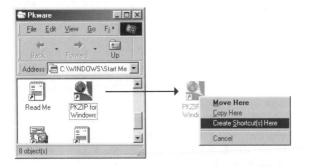

Figure 10.3 Creating a shortcut icon on the Windows desktop.

Now simply double-click on this icon to launch PKZip for Windows.

Figure 10.4 The PKZip window after launching the application.

Whatever method you use, the PKZip application window is displayed (see Figure 10.4).

With a keyboard shortcut

Right-click on the **Start** button and select **Open** in the menu. A window named **Start-up menu** appears on the screen. Double-click on the **Programs** icon, then on the **PKWare** icon. The previous window now contains all the icons of PKZip for Windows (see Figure 10.5).

1. Right-click on the **PKZip for Windows** icon and choose **Properties** in the context menu.

2. If necessary, select the **Shortcut** tab, click on the **Shortcut keys** text box and choose a keyboard shortcut with the **Ctrl**, **Alt** or **Shift** keys and an alphanumeric key, for example **Ctrl-Alt-P** (see Figure 10.6).

3. Confirm by clicking on the **OK** button.

You can now launch PKZip for Windows with the keyboard shortcut you have just defined, from whichever application you may be in.

Figure 10.5 The PKWare suite.

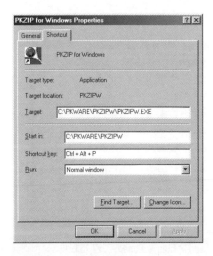

Figure 10.6 Applying a keyboard shortcut to the application.

The keyboard shortcut will only work if it does not conflict with the various keyboard shortcuts of the application you are running. For example, if your keyboard shortcut for PKZip for Windows is Alt-Shift-R, you will not be able to use the same one in Microsoft Word, as this in fact corresponds to the Rulers command in the View menu.

■ The PKZip window

PKZip is an **MDI** (*Multiple Document Interface*) application. In other words, you can open several archives at the same time in PKZip (see Figure 10.7). As we will see in the section "Two further methods of adding files to an archive", in Chapter 12, this feature allows files to be exchanged between two or more archives.

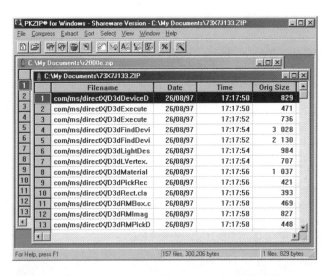

Figure 10.7 In this example, two ZIP files are open 73x7j133.ZIP and r2000e.ZIP.

In common with most Windows applications, PKZip has:

- a title bar
- a menu bar
- a toolbar
- a status bar.

The title bar

The title bar shows the name of the archive that is currently open. When several archives are open at the same time, the name of the active archive (that is, the one where the title bar is active) appears in the application title bar.

The menu bar

The menu bar provides access to all the application commands. Please note the following commands:

- **Open** and **New** in the **File** menu, with which you can respectively open an existing archive and create a new one
- **Convert** in the **File** menu, which makes the current archive self-extracting
- **Wizard** in the **File** menu, which accesses the wizard function. Check the section on "The PKZip Wizard"" in Chapter 11 for further information
- **Add Files** in the **Compress** menu, which adds files to the current archive
- **Delete Files** in the **Compress** menu, which deletes the file or files selected from the current archive
- **Preferences** in the **Compress** menu, which accesses the compression parameters
- **Open** in the **Extract** menu, which displays the highlighted file without having to decompress the archive
- **Extract Files** in the **Extract** menu, which decompresses the file or files of your choice

- **Test Files** in the **Extract** menu, which tests the integrity of the files in the current archive
- **Preferences** in the **Extract** menu, which accesses the decompression parameters
- **Index** in the **Help** menu, which accesses PKZip interactive help.

The toolbar

The toolbar makes access to the main menu commands easier:

Icon	Command	Equivalent function
	New in the **File** menu	Defines a new archive
	Open in the **File** menu	Opens an existing archive
	Add Files in the **Compress** menu	Adds one or more files to the current archive
	Extract Files in the **Extract** menu	Extracts one or more files from the current archive
	Delete Files in the **Compress** menu	Removes one or more files from the current archive
	Test Files in the **Extract** menu	Tests the integrity of files in the current archive

Icon	Command	Equivalent function
	All in the **Select** menu	Selects all the files in the current archive
	Clear all in the **Select** menu	Deselects all the files in the current archive
	By Filename in the **Select** menu	Selects one or more files of a specified type in the current archive
	By File Size in the **Select** menu	Selects one or more files in the current archive with a specified type
	By File Date in the **Select** menu	Selects one or more files in the current archive with a specified type
	Statistics in the **Compress** menu	Displays the number of files in the archive, their size before and after compression and the compression ratio
	Wizard in the **File** menu	Activates the Wizard function

The status bar

The status bar permanently displays various items of information concerning:

■ the menu commands where the toolbar icon is pointed

- the current archive
- the selected files in the archive.

In the example in Figure 10.8, the pointer is on the **Delete files** icon in the toolbar. The current archive contains fourteen files which, uncompressed, take up 750,072 bytes. The size of the three selected files is 196,608 bytes before compression.

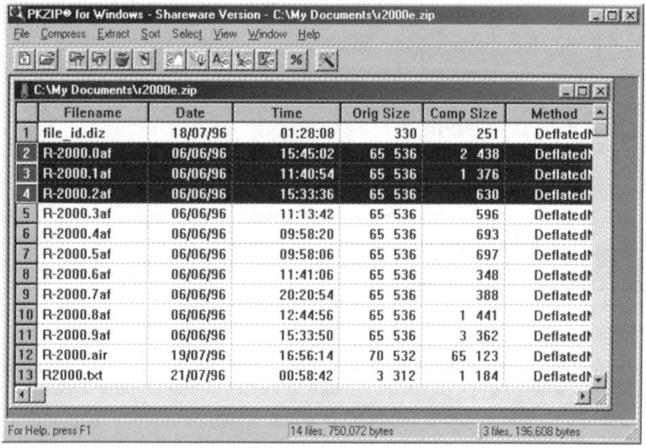
PKZIP® for Windows - Shareware Version - C:\My Documents\r2000e.zip
File Compress Extract Sort Select View Window Help
C:\My Documents\r2000e.zip
Filename Date Time Orig Size Comp Size Method
1 file_id.diz 18/07/96 01:28:08 330 251 Deflated
2 R-2000.0af 06/06/96 15:45:02 65 536 2 438 Deflated
3 R-2000.1af 06/06/96 11:40:54 65 536 1 376 Deflated
4 R-2000.2af 06/06/96 15:33:36 65 536 630 Deflated
5 R-2000.3af 06/06/96 11:13:42 65 536 596 Deflated
6 R-2000.4af 06/06/96 09:58:20 65 536 693 Deflated
7 R-2000.5af 06/06/96 09:58:06 65 536 697 Deflated
8 R-2000.6af 06/06/96 11:41:06 65 536 348 Deflated
9 R-2000.7af 06/06/96 20:20:54 65 536 388 Deflated
10 R-2000.8af 06/06/96 12:44:56 65 536 1 441 Deflated
11 R-2000.9af 06/06/96 15:33:50 65 536 3 362 Deflated
12 R-2000.air 19/07/96 16:56:14 70 532 65 123 Deflated
13 R2000.txt 21/07/96 00:58:42 3 312 1 184 Deflated
For Help, press F1
14 files, 750,072 bytes
3 files, 196,608 bytes

Figure 10.8 An example of how to use the status bar.

The work area

The work area is between the toolbar at the top of the window and the status bar at the bottom. The files contained in each open archive can be viewed in the windows which form part of the work area. Click on the maximise option to enlarge a window to its maximum size. If there are several open archives, toggle between them using the Windows menu commands or the **Ctrl-F6** keyboard shortcut.

■ Uninstalling PKZip

PKZip comes with an installation program. To run it, click on the **Start** button, then use the **Programs, PKWare** and then the **Uninstall** command. Uninstallation is carried out after confirmation.

■ Downloading the latest version of PKZip

At the time of writing, the 32-bit version of PKZip 2.60 was the latest version available. By the time you read this, there will probably be another version available.

To make sure, get on to **http://www.pkware.com/** and click on **PKZip, Command Line for Windows 95/NT** (see Figure 10.9).

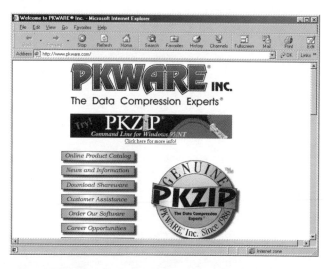

Figure 10.9 The PKWare Web site provides access to the latest versions of PKZip for Windows.

■ Buying the PKZip for Windows pack

Print out the purchase order for the PKZip for Windows pack from the **ORDER.TXT** file in the installation folder.

PKZip for Windows is distributed in the UK by PKWare Inc.:

PKWare Inc.
9025 N. Deerwood Drive
Brown Deer
WI USA 53223
Tel.: (414) 354-8699
Fax: (414) 354-8559
BBS: (414) 354-8670
Email: **sales@pkware.com**
Website: **http://www.pkware.com**

11

Basic use of PKZip

This lesson is dedicated to PKZip. You will learn to use its Wizard function to decompress an existing archive and create a new -archive, as well as to use its Classic mode to view the contents of an archive and decompress an existing archive.

■ The PKZip Wizard

If you have never compressed and decompressed files before, you will be glad of the PKZip Wizard function. Click on the **Wizard** button in PKZip toolbar or use the **Wizard** command in the **File** menu. Either of these actions displays the dialog box in Figure 11.1.

Select the first or the second option, depending on whether you want to decompress an archive or create a new one.

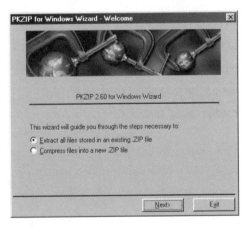

Figure 11.1 The PKZip Wizard simplifies the compression and decompression of files.

Decompressing an existing archive

Having selected **Extract all files stored in an existing ZIP file**, click on the **Next** button. Select the ZIP file to be decompressed (see Figure 11.2).

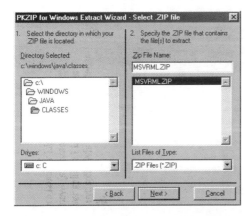

Figure 11.2 Choosing the folder containing the ZIP file, then selecting the ZIP file.

A click on the **Next** button, and the wizard displays the dialog box in Figure 11.3. Leave the option selected if you want to restore the tree structure saved in the ZIP file. Enter a password if the archive is protected. Click on the **Next** button.

The next step will be to define a destination folder where the ZIP file can be decompressed. By default, this will be the same folder as the one in the archive. Chose another drive or folder, if you so want, and click on the **Next** button. The archive is soon decompressed. Click on the **Done** button then on the **Close** button. The PKZip window contains the list of the files which have just been decompressed (see Figure 11.4).

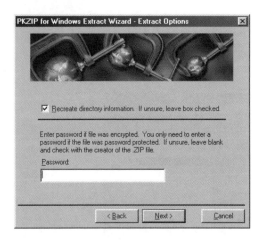

Figure 11.3 Restoring the tree structure and entering the password.

	Filename	Date	Time	Orig Size	Comp S
1	com/ms/msvrml2c/ArrayCon	14/10/1997	14:58:26	570	
2	com/ms/msvrml2c/Field.clas	14/10/1997	14:58:22	2 349	2
3	com/ms/msvrml2c/javacom/	14/10/1997	14:58:08	487	
4	com/ms/msvrml2c/javacom/	14/10/1997	14:58:08	880	
5	com/ms/msvrml2c/javacom/	14/10/1997	14:58:08	667	
6	com/ms/msvrml2c/javacom/	14/10/1997	14:58:08	645	
7	com/ms/msvrml2c/javacom/	14/10/1997	14:58:08	335	
8	com/ms/msvrml2c/javacom/	14/10/1997	14:58:08	422	
9	com/ms/msvrml2c/javacom/	14/10/1997	14:58:08	356	
10	com/ms/msvrml2c/javacom/	14/10/1997	14:58:08	478	
11	com/ms/msvrml2c/javacom/	14/10/1997	14:58:08	332	
12	com/ms/msvrml2c/javacom/	14/10/1997	14:58:08	2 447	2
13	com/ms/msvrml2c/javacom/	14/10/1997	14:58:08	6 850	6
14	com/ms/msvrml2c/javacom/	14/10/1997	14:58:08	5 322	5

For Help, press F1 — 361 files, 259,877 bytes — 1 files, 570 bytes

Figure 11.4 The PKZip window after decompression.

Defining a new archive

To define a new archive with the Wizard, select the **Compress files into a new .ZIP file** option, then click on the **Next** button. You are prompted to specify the drive and the folder in which you want to create the ZIP file, as well as the name of the ZIP file (see Figure 11.5).

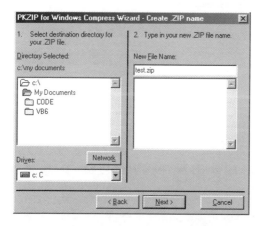

Figure 11.5 Defining the path and the name of the ZIP file.

Now you must select the files or folders to be compressed. To add a folder to the archive, select it in the first list box and click on the **Add Directory** button. To add one or more files to the archive, choose the folder which contains the files in the first list box, carry out your selection in the second list box and click on the **Add Files** button. In the example in Figure 11.6, the **h:\ssm\archives** folder as well as images 10 to 15 in the **h:\ssm\images** folder have been selected.

Simply click on the **Compress now** button to start compression. When the archive has been created, its contents are displayed in the PKZip window (see Figure 11.7).

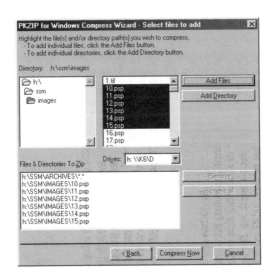

Figure 11.6 Choosing the folders and files to be stored in the archive.

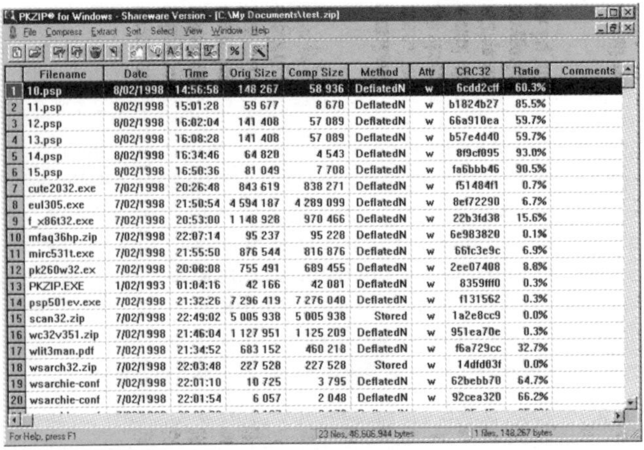

Figure 11.7 The contents of the new archive.

In this window, the following information is displayed for each compressed file:

- date and time of creation
- size before and after compression
- compression method used
- compression ratio.

■ Viewing the contents of an archive

To view the files contained in a ZIP, UUE, XXE, HQX, MIM, MME, TAR, GZ or TGZ archive, simply open the archive itself. To do this, you can:

- click on the **Open** button in the toolbar
- use the **Open** command in the **File** menu
- use the **Ctrl-O** keyboard shortcut.

Whichever method you use, after opening an archive, the PKZip window will resemble the one in Figure 11.8.

	Filename	Date	Time	Orig Size	Comp Size	Method	Attr	CRC32
7	part13	06/12/1995	07:23:00	59 878	19 651	DeflatedN	w	566fe102
8	part14	06/12/1995	07:24:00	60 071	18 752	DeflatedN	w	4616098c
9	part15	06/12/1995	07:24:00	59 756	19 642	DeflatedN	w	eb1ebcef
10	part16	06/12/1995	07:24:00	59 635	18 829	DeflatedN	w	d2d10d08
11	part17	06/12/1995	07:25:00	59 542	18 196	DeflatedN	w	8e53acbf
12	part18	06/12/1995	07:26:00	59 776	18 525	DeflatedN	w	edaa594e
13	part19	06/12/1995	07:26:00	59 438	18 328	DeflatedN	w	971e411f
14	part2	06/12/1995	07:12:00	59 717	18 488	DeflatedN	w	51fdfc99

Figure 11.8 Several items of information appear for each file.

The following information is displayed for each file:

- the name of the file: **Filename**
- date and time of creation of the compressed file: **Date and Time**
- the size of the file before compression: **Orig Size**
- the size of the compressed file: **Comp Size**
- the compression method: **Method**
- the file attributes (read only, archive, hidden file, system file): **Attr**
- the CRC value calculated during the CRC 32 verification routine: **CRC-32**
- the reduction percentage: **Ratio**
- comments, if applicable: **Comments**.

If you want, you can vary the type of information displayed for each file. Use the **Preferences** command in the **View** menu and deactivate one or more options in the **Display** option group (see Figure 11.9).

Figure 11.9 Choosing the information displayed in the PKZip window.

To view a file, you do not need to decompress the archive. Double-click on it in the PKZip window. The file will be displayed in the associated application.

 *To be able to open a file in the appropriate application, Windows 95 and 98 associate types of files with applications. In most cases, these associations are carried out during the installation procedure. If you want, you can define new associations manually. Open My Computer or Explorer. Use the **Options** command in the **Display** menu. Select the **File type** tab. Click on the **New type** button and complete the **Add new type of files** dialog box. In the example in Figure 11.10, the files with the **.DIZ** extension are opened in Windows Notepad.*

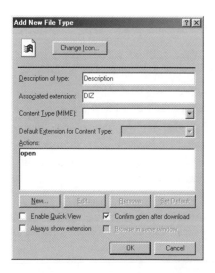

Figure 11.10 Defining a new association between files with the .DIZ extension and Notepad.

In this example, you want to open the file with the .DIZ extension on which you have double-clicked. To define the

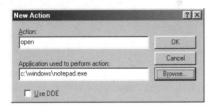

**Figure 11.11 The file on which you have
double-clicked will be opened in Notepad.**

action to be carried out, click on the **New** button and specify the program to be used (see Figure 11.11).

■ Another method of viewing an archive

If the PKZip window is open, you can still use the Windows
drag and drop function to view the contents of an archive:

1. Display the archive whose contents you want to view in
   My Computer or in Windows 95/98 Explorer.

2. Click on the archive, keeping the left mouse button
   pressed and move the archive to the PKZip window.

3. Release the left mouse button. The contents of the archive
   is displayed in the PKZip window.

If you are not very good at dragging and dropping, you can
right-click on the archive icon in My Computer or in
Windows Explorer and select **Open** to open the archive in
PKZip.

 *This command only appears if the PKZip application has been
associated to the ZIP extension. If it has not been associated,
simply use the **Associate to ZIP** command in the PKZip **File**
menu to remedy the situation.*

■ Decompressing an archive

If you have already decompressed a number of ZIP files, you will probably prefer not to use the Wizard.

To restore the files contained in an existing archive, follow these six steps:

1. Open the **ZIP, UUE, XXE, MIM, MME, HQX, TAR, TGZ** or **GZ** archive. To do this, click on the **Open** button in the toolbar, use the **Open** command in the **File** menu or use the keyboard shortcut **Ctrl-O**.

2. Select the files to be extracted. Remember that, to select several consecutive files, you only need to click on the first and on the last one while keeping the **Shift** key depressed. If the files to be selected are not consecutive, select them by keeping the **Ctrl** key depressed. You will not need the second step if you want to decompress all the files in the archive.

3. Display the **Extract** dialog box. To do this, you can click with the right mouse button on one of the files listed in the archive and select **Extract** in the context menu, or use the **Extract files** command in the **Extract** menu.

4. Select the destination folder by entering its path in the **Disk** text box (if necessary, use the **Browse** button to simplify entering the path). If the destination folder does not exist, you must create it by clicking on the **Create Directory** button before selecting it in the **Disk** text box.

5. Enter a password if the archive is password-protected.

6. Click on the **Extract** button to extract the files.

The **Preferences** button accesses a number of interesting options (see Figure 11.12).

Figure 11.12 Decompression options.

You will use:

- The **Extract options** option group to determine the actions to be carried out when some of the decompressed files already exist in the destination folder. You can choose between:

  - **Overwrite** to replace existing files with the files that are about to be decompressed.

  - **Update** so that the decompression process only updates the existing files.

  - **Update & New** to extract new files and replace the existing files with the most recently created files in the archive.

  - **Prompt user** to ask for instructions on to what to do when a file in the archive has the same name as an existing file.

- The **Restore attributes** option group to specify if the decompressed files should retain their read only, cached and/or system attributes.

- The **Create directory** option to determine if tree structure saved in an archive must be restored when decompressing.

Self-extracting archives

To decompress a self-extracting archive, simply double-click on it in My Computer or Explorer. The dialog box shown in Figure 11.13 is displayed.

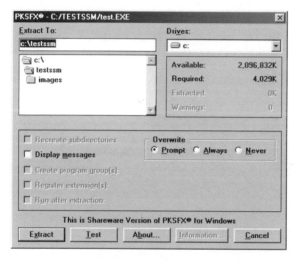

Figure 11.13 Decompressing a self-extracting archive.

Select the decompression drive and folder. The required space and the available space are displayed at the top of the dialog box.

Choose one or more options located at the bottom of the window depending on what you want to achieve. You can also click on the **Test** button to test the integrity of the archive or directly on the **Extract** button to start decompressing.

■ Another method of decompressing an existing archive

Archives can also be decompressed from My Computer or Windows Explorer. Find the **ZIP, EXE, UUE, XXE, MIM, MME, HQX, TAR, TGZ** or **GZ** archive you want to decompress. Right-click on its icon and select **Extract To** in the context menu. The archive will be automatically opened in PKZip and the **Extract** dialog box will allow you to specify the folder into which you want to save the decompressed files (see Figure 11.14).

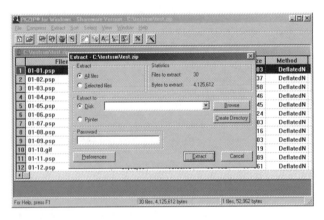

Figure 11.14 Compression options.

 *The **Extract To** command appears in the context menu only if the PKZip application has been associated to the ZIP extension. If it has not, simply use the **Associate to ZIP** command in PKZip **File** menu to remedy the situation.*

12
Advanced use of PKZip

■ ■ ■ ■ ■ ■ ■ ■ ■ ■ ■ ■ ■ ■ ■ ■ ■ ■ ■ ■

Creating a new archive

Adding files to an existing archive

Deleting files from an existing archive

Viewing the contents of files in an archive without decompressing it

Defining a self-extracting archive

Protecting an archive with a password

Creating an archive spanning several diskettes

Reviewing the Zip files in your system

The following pages show you how to use the advanced comment compression functions in PKZip in Classic mode. You will also learn how to define a self-extracting archive, how to protect an archive with a password and how to create an archive on several diskettes.

■ Creating a new archive

Creating a new archive is very simple. Just follow these four steps:

1. Click on the **New** button in the toolbar, use the **New** command in the **File** menu or press **Ctrl-N**.

2. Enter the archive path and name in the **Save as** dialog box, then click on the **Save** button.

3. Select the files and folders to be placed in the archive. To add a folder to the archive, select it in the first list box and click on the **Add Directory** button. To add one or more files to the archive, choose the folder containing the files in the first list box, carry out the selection in the second list box while keeping the **Ctrl** key pressed on the keyboard, then click on the **Add Files** button.

4. Click on the **OK** button to create the archive. When the operation is completed, the compressed files will appear in the PKZip window.

Specifying compression parameters

The **Preferences** button accesses various compression parameters (see Figure 12.1).

The **Compression option** group allows you to choose the compression ratio. The higher the compression ratio, the longer it takes to compress the archive. The **Normal** value is a good compromise between speed and compression ratio.

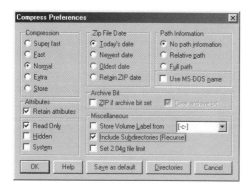

Figure 12.1 Compression options.

The table below provides an indication of the size of ZIP files obtained by selecting the five suggested values in the **Compression** drop down list. The compressed files in this example are PSP images in 16 million colours, saved from Paint Shop Pro.

Compression type	File size	Compression ratio in bytes
Super Fast	1,438,728	2.77
Fast	1,274,793	3.12
Normal	1,218,591	3.27
Extra	1,206,926	3.30
Store	3,985,891	0

The Zip File Date option group allows you to choose the date information shown for the new archive. You can choose:

- **Today's date** to show the archive system date

- **Newest date** to show the date of the most recent file in the archive

- **Oldest date** to show the date of the oldest file in the archive.

The **Path Information** option group indicates if the files path must be saved in the archive. Select:

- **No path information** if you do not want to save the files path

- **Relative path** if you want to save the path which you have set manually

- **Full path** to save the complete path for each file.

Leave the **Use MS-DOS name** option deactivated, unless you want to create an archive which is compatible with short file-names (8-character names with 3-character file extensions). In this case, all long filenames in the archive will be truncated.

The **Attributes** option group defines the file attributes to be saved in the archive. If you choose the **Retain attributes** option, all the files will be saved with their current attributes. Choose one or more of the **Read-Only, Hidden** and/or **System** options according to whether you want to save the files as read only, hidden and/or system.

Finally, the **Miscellaneous** option group accesses three unclassified options:

- **Store Volume Label.** If you select this option, the specified drive name will also be stored in the archive

- **Include Subdirectories (Recurse).** If a folder contains one or more subfolders that need to be included in the archive, they can be included in the archive with this option

- **Set 204g file limit.** Choose this option if you want your archives to be compatible with PKZip version 2.04g. The

maximum number of files which can be placed in an
archive ranges from 65,535 to 16,383.

■ Another method of creating an archive

It is also possible to create a PKZip archive from My
Computer or Windows Explorer. This is how you do it:

1. Right-click on an empty part of My Computer or Explorer
   and select **New/PKZip File** in the context menu. This
   action creates a new icon called **New PKZip File**.

2. Modify the name of this archive by right-clicking on the
   icon and selecting **Rename** in the context menu.

3. Double-click on the icon you have just created. The new
   archive is opened in PKZip. Simply add the files of your
   choice using the methods shown in the next section.

■ Adding files to an existing archive

After opening the archive to which you want to add files,
click on the **Add files** button in the toolbar (or use the **Add
files** command in the **Compress** menu) and specify the folders and/or files to be added to the archive. As shown in Figure
12.2, you can choose one of three methods.

By selecting the option:

- **Add files.** The selected files are added to the archive
- **Update files.** The selected files update the files in the
  archive, if there are any
- **Add & Update files.** The selected files are added to the
  archive if they do not exist already. Otherwise they replace
  the existing files.

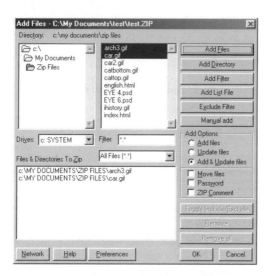

Figure 12.2 The Add Options option group proposes
three methods for adding.

■ Two more methods of adding files to an archive

You can add files to an open archive by dragging and dropping from My Computer or Explorer, just as you can in
WinZip. This is how you do it:

1. Click on the **Open** button in the PKZip toolbar and specify the name of the archive to which you want to add the
files.

2. View the files you want to add to the archive with My
Computer or Windows Explorer.

3. Select these files by clicking on them, with the **Ctrl** key
pressed.

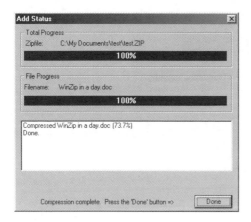

Figure 12.3 Adding a file to the archive by dragging and dropping.

4. Move the selected files to the PKZip window. A dialog box will show you the nature of the add operation (see Figure 12.3).

PKZip can open several archives at the same time. To copy or move files from one open archive to another, do the following:

1. Open all the archives from which you want to copy/transfer files.

2. Select the file or files to be copied/transferred by clicking on them, with the **Ctrl** key pressed if necessary.

3. Right-click on the selection and choose:

   ■ **Copy To** in the context menu to copy the selected files into one of the other open archives.

   ■ **Move To** in the context menu to copy the selected files in one of the other open archives and remove it from the original archive.

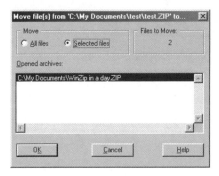

Figure 12.4 Moving files between archives.

4. The dialog box shown in Figure 12.4 is displayed. Choose the destination archive in the list box and click on the **OK** button.

■ Removing files from an existing archive

Open the archive to be modified and select the files to be removed. Remember that, to select several consecutive files, simply click on the first and then on the last file while keeping the **Shift** key pressed. If the files to be selected are not consecutive, select them while keeping the **Ctrl** key pressed. When all the files to be removed are highlighted, click on the **Delete files** button in the toolbar, press the **Del** key on the keyboard or use the **Delete files** command in the **Compress** menu. The selected files are deleted after confirmation.

 *For quick selection of a set of files with specific criteria for name, size or creation date, use the **Select** menu commands.*

■ Viewing the contents of files in an archive without decompressing it

It is not necessary to decompress an archive to view the contents of one of its files. Open the archive by double-clicking on it in My Computer or in Explorer (the assumption here is that the files with the .ZIP extensions are associated to the PKZip program). In the **PKZip for Windows** window, right-click on the file you want to view and select **Open** in the context menu. If the file extension is associated to an application, this is then launched and the file is opened.

Otherwise, a dialog box named **Open With** will prompt you to specify the name of the program to be used for opening the file (see Figure 12.5).

Figure 12.5 Specify the name of the application in which you want to open the file.

■ Defining a self-extracting archive

If you are sending out compressed files to users who do not have the appropriate decompression software, it is better to send them self-extracting archives.

Self-extracting archives are executable programs. To access the files included, simply run them.

PKZip can change an existing ZIP file to a self-extracting archive, but it can also create a self-extracting archive directly.

To define a self-extracting file from an existing archive, follow these steps:

1. Open the archive to be changed by clicking on the **Open** button in the toolbar (you can also use the **Open** command in the **File** menu or use the keyboard shortcut **Ctrl-O** to achieve the same results).

2. Use the **Convert** command in the **File** menu. Select **PKSFX WIN16 File** in the **Type** drop down list.

3. Define the name of the self-extracting archive in the **Name** text box and confirm. This action displays the dialog box shown in Figure 12.6. Enter the name of the destination folder in the **Extract To** text box. Then choose **Recreate subdirectories** if the archive contains one or more subfolders, the structure of which needs to be preserved when

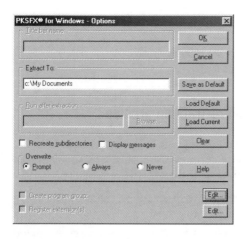

Figure 12.6 Defining the destination folder for the self-extracting archive.

decompressing. Confirm by clicking on the **OK** button. The archive is then saved on the hard disk.

The shareware version of PKZip provides the choice of three formats for self-extracting archives:

◆ ***PKSFX DOSFULL**: MS-DOS traditional format*

◆ ***PKSFX JRDOS**: MS-DOS compact format, with a lower performance*

◆ ***PKSFX WIN16**: format for Windows 3.1 and later versions. Windows 95/98 supports long filenames.*

If you register your version of PKZip, you will also be able to create files in WIN32 format which can be run under Windows 95/98/NT (Intel, Alpha and PowerPC).

As mentioned earlier, you can also create self-extracting archives directly. This is how you do it:

1. Click on the **New** button in the PKZip toolbar.
2. Select **PKSFX WIN16 File** in the **Type** drop down list, enter the name of the self-extracting archive in the **Name** text box and confirm.
3. Select the files and/or folders to be placed in the archive as per usual.
4. Indicate the destination folder and confirm.

A self-extracting archive containing the selected files is created.

■ Password-protecting an archive

It may be necessary to protect some archives with a password. A password-protected archive cannot be decompressed without the correct password. If you provide the recipient with the password, you will be sure that your data can only be used by an authorised party.

Figure 12.7 Attaching a password to the current archive.

To attach a password to a ZIP or EXE archive, choose the **Password** option in the **Add Files** dialog box. A dialog box then prompts you to enter the password (see Figure 12.7). Do not forget the password: nobody will be able to carry out the decompression without this password.

■ Creating an archive spanning several diskettes

ZIP or EXE archives are occasionally too large to be stored in full on one diskette. In this case, you need to put them on several diskettes. PKZip does it automatically if the disk on which the archive is to be stored is a removable drive or a diskette drive.

When decompressing, PKZip will prompt the user to insert the diskettes containing the archive one after another.

■ Reviewing the ZIP files in your system

PKZip cannot review the archives stored in your system in the same way that WinZip can. Windows 95 and 98, on the other hand, are quite good at this. Click on the **Start** button

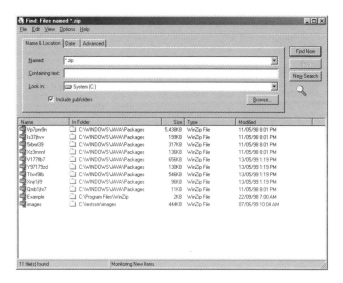

Figure 12.8 The search window in Windows.

and select **Search** in the menu, then **Files or folders**. Enter the specified type "*.zip" in the **Named** text box, choose the drive or drives and/or folder or folders to be searched in the **Search in** text box and click on the **Search now** button.

Within a few seconds, a **Search** dialog box resembling that shown in Figure 12.8 appears.

The files may be sorted by name, folder, size, type or date of creation/last modification by clicking on the corresponding headings.

To open one of the listed archives, right-click on its name and select the **Open** command in the context menu. You may also choose the **Extract to** command to extract its contents and place it into the folder of your choice or **Test** to test the integrity of the files included in the archive.

Index

....